D0380966

FATHER GUY MURNIG

CONCILIUM
Religion in the Seventies

CONCILIUM
Religion in the Seventies

EDITORIAL DIRECTORS: Edward Schillebeeckx (Dogma) •
Herman Schmidt (Liturgy) • Alois Müller (Pastoral) •
Hans Küng (Ecumenism) • Franz Böckle (Moral Theology) •
Johannes B. Metz (Church and World) • Roger Aubert (Church
History) • Teodoro Jiménez Urresti (Canon Law) • Christian
Duquoc (Spirituality) • Pierre Benoît and Roland Murphy
(Scripture)

CONSULTING EDITORS: Marie-Dominique Chenu • ✠Carlo
Colombo • Yves Congar • Andrew Greeley • Jorge Mejía •
Karl Rahner • Roberto Tucci

EXECUTIVE SECRETARY: (Awaiting new appointment),
Arksteestraat 3–5, Nijmegen, The Netherlands

Volume 73: Pastoral

EDITORIAL BOARD: Alois Müller • Norbert Greinacher •
Wilhelm van Bekkum • Martin Ekwa • Rafael Espin Lastra •
Adolf Exeler • Henri-Marie Féret • Casiano Floristán •
Domenico Grasso • Alfonso Gregory • Frans Haarsma •
Adrian Hastings • Johannes Hofinger • François Houtart •
Jan Kerkhofs • James Killgallon • Ferdinand Klostermann •
Jean Le Du • François Lepargneur • Angelo Macchi •
Józef Majka • Barthélemy Nyom • Juán Ochagavia •
Gustavo Perez Ramirez • Emile Pin • Karl Rahner •
José Rodriguez Medina • Heinz Schuster • Gerard Sloyan •
Anthony Spencer • Theodore Steeman • Rolf Zerfass

ONGOING REFORM OF THE CHURCH

Edited by
Alois Muller
and Norbert Greinacher

Herder and Herder

1972
HERDER AND HERDER NEW YORK
232 Madison Avenue, New York 10016

Cum approbatione Ecclesiastica

Library of Congress Catalog Card Number: 71–185749
Copyright © 1972 by Herder and Herder, Inc. and Stichting Concilium.
All rights reserved. Nothing contained in this publication shall be reproduced
and/or made public by means of print, photographic print, microfilm, or in
any other manner without the previous consent of the Stichting Concilium
and the publishers.

Printed in the United States

CONTENTS

PART II

DOCUMENTATION

SOME EXAMPLES OF REFORM IN LOCAL CHURCHES

Editorial

PROPHETIC voices within and without the Church have for a long time stressed the need for reform in the Catholic Church. Since the last Council, the necessity of such a reform has also entered the consciousness of broad circles inside the Church and has become the "horizon" of the concept of the Church today.

Yet in the post-conciliar period there has been considerable evidence of resistance to such a movement. Opinions are divided—but not only in regard to the exact nature of individual reforms. There are also questions regarding how far reforms can really go, in what way, through what mechanisms, and within what period of time they are to take effect. Behind all this, however, there is the question of what church reform is in general, and what ends it ought to serve. Admittedly "pre-conciliar" viewpoints according to which mention of the *Ecclesia semper reformanda* was prohibited under suspicion of heresy were nullified by the Council itself. Yet it was only (and precisely) with the commencement of the conciliar reforms that the really profound dimension of the problem was revealed. This is the age which has recognized that problems concerning the Church cannot be resolved solely on a theological basis. The Church is a human institution; in it the laws take effect which condition every institution, and which are analysed by behavioural science. Perhaps there is an obstacle to a real breakthrough of reform inherent in that false evaluation of the Church that would think to do it justice by a purely theological form of conceptualization, while ignoring that it is subject to the laws of human existence, and overlooking its very historicity.

Church reform, which was experienced in the period of the Council as an overdue and happy change, has now become a weary business when the powers who oppose it appear without any mask, and the forces of reform have largely lost their joy and courage. The Church is becoming polarized. Many questions also have to be asked about the reform of the Church which were discovered only in the process of reform. Hence church reform becomes a problem of practical theology *par excellence*.

This issue of *Concilium* poses questions and conducts a discussion. Perhaps it is already church reform in process, since it presents thoughts not only about diverse things but from diverse thinkers. It has to be acknowledged that a church reform which wants to overcome a dangerous tendency to split simply has to take this plurality of approaches into account. A theory of church reform has to tackle the question from different angles. First of all there is the problem of the involvement of the Church as an institution in a particular society. There is also the question whether church structures, like doctrines, may not be threatened by "falsity", so that a reform in this sense is theologically inevitable. This is again an occasion to remember the dialectic of spirit and institution behind every process of reform. Such problems help to locate the fundamental question of what exactly are the theological grounds, occasions and goals of church reform.

But a church reform also presupposes a change of consciousness as much as it induces it; it raises the question of a locally differentiated and therefore not centrally controllable reform, and of the apparent attitude of the Church to the notion of conflict. It would be tragic if the will to church reform were to succumb to the present difficulties. The illumination and enunciation of prerequisites, conditions and problems should comprise the service to the Church that will allow it (once again) to become a Church that reforms with joy.

ALOIS MÜLLER
NORBERT GREINACHER

PART I
ARTICLES

Thomas F. O'Dea

Church Reform and Society in Evolutionary Perspective

I. Introduction

The Catholic Church entered the modern period under in-
auspicious conditions. It was increasingly removed from the concerns of modern men and its stance was characterized by two
counter-positions: Counter Reformation after 1521, and after
1789 Counter Revolution. Its attitude was markedly reserved towards the development of science. The Church had been the
progenitor of the older civilization and that order had supplied
a cultural milieu that provided a supportive credibility structure
for the act and habit of faith. The modern period changed all
this. The over-arching Christian culture and the central position
of the Church were destroyed. Pluralism, rapid change and open
hostility created a new environment with which the Church had
to cope. The Church behaved increasingly like a gigantic sect in
the face of this situation, attempting to defend not only its faith
but the cultural and social contexts that had supported it in the
past. It saw the modern situation in terms of what has been
called the "root idea of Pio Nono";[1] it considered Western Europe
to have taken the wrong road, while secular opinion saw the
Church as an obsolete historical survival. Consequently the
Church became more and more authoritarian in structure and
increasingly constrained in its attitudes. Yet throughout this

[1] E. E. Y. Hales, *Pope John and His Revolution* (Garden City, New
York, 1965), p. 50.

travail it maintained its inner religious authenticity and remained a "school of sanctity".[2]

These developments have as much to do with what is happening in society as with what goes on in the Church. After a century and a half of unsuccessful minority effort,[3] Vatican II undid the stance of Counter Reformation and Counter Revolution and proclaimed the freedom of scientific inquiry.[4] These developments, too, are part of a larger Church-society dialectic. Today's world is in crisis, and while its chaos threatens the Church in a new way, it is less hostile in significant respects than was the world of the previous period. It presents a situation full of potential for both creation and destruction. For the Church it is indeed the best and the worst of times. Can the Church achieve genuine reform and be the outward sign and institutional means of man's relation to Transcendence? Or must it now become a sect bearing witness as a lonely pilgrim to its own vertical dimension? Or is there another way—a way yet unrecognized and unexplored? We shall discuss these questions, although no one can yet answer them.

II. Church and Society: The Sociological Context of Ecclesial Existence

Every society is an acted-out answer to the implicit question: What ought man to be doing on this earth, being the kind of being that he is? Acted out in specific historically conditioned ways, it elicits and brings to realization certain human possibilities, while neglecting and even repressing others. It is acted out in response to a given environment and involves a specific division of labour and reward. Even within one societal order, one answer to the constitutive question, there are different degrees of expression and inhibition, of satisfaction and deprivation, imposed upon men. The environment is not composed simply of things ready to hand for man's use; it is a total world

[2] Henri Daniel-Rops, *The Catholic Reformation*, Vol. II (Garden City, New York, 1964), p. 163.

[3] See Thomas F. O'Dea, *The Catholic Crisis* (Boston, 1969), ch. III, pp. 38–89.

[4] *Gaudium et Spes*, art. 36.

and beyond it lies ultimate reality. God and man, world and society, constitute a basic quarternary structure in which all men participate. The sociologist may distinguish here four foci of response around which crystallize orientations and institutions. First, there is a relational focus that elicits a personal response. This involves both psycho-sexual elements and the acting out of archetypal relationships.[5] Second, there is an environmental focus involving specific tasks necessary for the survival and enhancement of life. Long the concern of the lowly, modern technology transformed it into a mighty dynamic force. Third, there is the realm of power, authority and community, long a favourite sphere for the acting out of the human drama. Finally, there is the religious sphere—the drama of salvation—in which men are related to a Beyond.

Man's relation to these invariant points of reference is not simply that of manipulating means for the attainment of ends. Rather he behaves as a dramatic actor. He acts out a drama that expresses his hopes and fears, his ambitions and his defences, in a play parts of whose stage setting and plot are inherited from the past, and parts of which are constructed in the course of the drama itself. In such acting out man shapes himself and establishes his society. He evolves a patterned allocation of functions, facilities and rewards that provides the context for his life and he sees it as part of an overall order whose legitimacy is guaranteed by the Beyond. In archaic societies the responses to these foci are fused and the constitutive symbolism evolved consists of a compact mythology whose elements are multivalent. In biblical religion, these responses have become differentiated. The first has been largely repressed since the victory of Yahwism over Baalism so far as its religious expression is concerned. However, this suppression has pushed into the unconscious elements that can arise to threaten the stability of individuals and society. The second—work—Christianity has recognized as necessary and worthy; the Christian ages bequeathed to the modern world a conception of the dignity of labour unknown in classical antiquity. Christianity also, not without trouble, recognized the legitimacy of the civil power. The prophetic experience in Israel

[5] See the works of Freud and Jung.

de-sacralized the social order, as may be seen in the Book of Amos, and drew a sharp distinction between patriotism and duty before God, as may be seen in the Book of Jeremiah. Jewish and Christian experience confirmed these differentiations.

With the decline of antiquity, Europe faced two new environmental challenges, the need for civil order and the provision of food and fibre. The first was solved by feudalism, by the rise of the Holy Roman Empire and the medieval monarchies. The second was met by the institution of manorialism, which although it consigned a majority to serfdom provided the economic base for civilization. These institutions developed out of the responses of men to concrete environmental problems. Had not the Church been present, these men would also have evolved indigenous religious institutions. However, the Church came into this situation, and brought its own institutional forms with it.

By the year 200, the Church had become an established structure, with its social, ideational and ritual forms increasingly fixed. In the spirit of the age its gaze was inward and heavenward; it was a community of the withdrawn awaiting the parousia. In its sacramental life it experienced and re-enacted the vertical dimension of man's relation to Transcendence. Ironically, this Church proved to be the only culturally vital entity to survive the chaos of the fall. As such it brought to the new Europe aborning not only its vision and its established forms but the remaining culture of the old civilization. It supplied the moral education that enabled Europe to rise and the higher education—based upon the study of the Latin authors and the Fathers —that enabled it to reassimilate the ancient heritage.

The Church shaped the religious needs of European man and made them of pre-eminent importance. Hence a third function became the most significant one, the pursuit and maintenance of the Christian relationship between God and man. The institutional embodiment of that was the Church itself. The fourth focus had been raised to a magnitude of importance that dwarfed the others in comparison. The Church's other-worldly orientation was increased by the difficult conditions of the Dark Ages, 700–1100. Indeed, the Church at that time not only embodied the religious vocation, but offered the most attractive life for men of sensitivity.

Sponsor of the new civilization, the Church, in Tillich's words, became the schoolmistress of Europe until the fourteenth century. But its other-worldliness and its fixity of form were causes of difficulty. All institutions are subject to the dilemma of mixed motivation. An institution provides a stable context for life because it can elicit behind its aims and practices not only idealistic but material and self-interested motivation. This contains its own dangers, however, for it can corrupt leadership and often in subtle ways.[6] This happened to the Church, which while remaining too other-worldly to do justice to rising lay aspirations was at the same time sufficiently caught in the web of vested interests to be this-worldly in a pragmatic sense and therefore unable to reform itself.

The high Middle Ages saw the rise of trade and towns and the emergence of lay middle classes. The cities of the Middle Ages already exhibited the lay religiosity that would lead to the Reformation and the lay spirit that would issue in the Renaissance.[7] What had begun was a commercial revolution that by the seventeenth century would alter drastically the character of European life. Commerce made men this-worldly and tended to quantify values.[8] The medieval university gave rise to science, which did in the intellectual realm what commerce did for urban life. It reduced the world of experience to "secondary characteristics" and made the world of mathematical abstraction the "really real". The two combined to "disenchant" the world and "demythologize" thought: that is, to make those spheres of life that did not fit into the abstractions of science or the calculations of business appear to be epistemologically suspect. The *philosophes* popularized science and thereby provided an ideology for the middle classes, whose way of life rendered them susceptible to its attractions. Moreover, this popularization was the work of literary men who left out the original religious attitudes of many of the great pioneers of science. The increase in wealth derived from commerce made this-worldly values more available and more attractive and the set other-worldliness of the Church

[6] See Thomas F. O'Dea, *Sociology and the Study of Religion* (New York, 1970), pp. 240–54.

[7] Henri Pirenne, *Medieval Cities* (Garden City, N.Y.), pp. 153–67.

[8] Karl Polanyi, *The Great Transformation* (Boston, 1957).

together with its quite worldly vested interests made it difficult for it to handle the new problems.

The Reformation came early in these developments. It represented an attempt to renew the religious life outside the now rigid structures, ideational, structural and liturgical, of the Catholic Church. But in the long run its unintended consequences hastened secularization. The Catholic Church was pushed from its former central position and alienated from the basic forward thrust of modern Western society. Its fixed forms had been unable either to contain or to channel the new energies, and they consequently found expression in forms that were at first anti-ecclesiastical, and later on anti-Christian: "During the middle ages the ecclesiastical institution included and formed human society; but from the beginning of the fourteenth century society slowly began to assert its independence." There evolved a situation characterized by "a kind of divorce between a community of men who were hardly the faithful any longer and an institution of clerics whose problems, activities, interests, language were no longer those of the living human community". By the middle of the twentieth century "the system and forms of the institution were in a way hiding the profound mystery of the Church".[9]

III. The Church, Relevance and Relativity

This brief outline of a complex situation indicates much deserving of study and reflection in relation to reform. Reform must be seen in the context of Church and society. Even when the Church is alienated from society, its alienation is conditioned by its societal situation. The perennial Church-society relationship assumes new forms and new meaning in our day. Today the whole world is undergoing an enormous transformation whose outcome no one can see. Vatican II recognized the crisis of the contemporary world, but it characterized it as a "crisis of growth" and offered a rather optimistic diagnosis.[10] Other diagnoses have been more pessimistic. At any rate, because of technology and the communications revolution, and the concomitant rising

[9] Yves M. J. Congar, *Lay People in the Church* (Westminster, Maryland, 1957), pp. 41, 51.
[10] *Gaudium et Spes*, art. 4.

aspirations of new peoples and new strata, a totally new situation now exists. Traditional societies are doomed to extinction and there takes place a rapid erosion of traditional enclaves in all societies. The Church must exist in the new situation differently from the way it existed in the medieval Catholic civilization, or in the modern society of the last four centuries, in which it lived increasingly in a state of siege. Once before, however, the Church lived in an urban society in crisis; the early Church in the Graeco-Roman world existed in a society that resembled our own, although today a dynamic technology and dynamic human aspirations introduce crucial differences.

Reform of the Church is not to be confused with superficial accommodation to the "secular city". Indeed, withdrawal proved to be the successful form of response for the early Church. The Church cannot avoid being conditioned, but it must strive to preserve what is essential and to emphasize its vertical dimension. It must never simply become adjusted or "contemporary" or "relevant". To abandon the healthy disarticulation that is the normal condition of religions of transcendence—an unadjustment to be seen even in the heyday of the Davidic and Solomonic kingdom—would be to disfigure the Church. It would be to introduce a truncation in the opposite direction from that which was imposed by the integralism and semi-integralism of the previous period. The search for authentic Catholic expression and reformulation is therefore a difficult one, and it has merely begun. It will require that Catholics combine effort and a sense of urgency with fortitude and patience—and have faith and hope.

IV. The Dialectic of Church and Society

Central to the life of the Church is the vertical dimension of relationship to the transcendent God and the indwelling of the Spirit that sustains it. This is true regardless whether we emphasize a conception of the Church as the "pilgrim people of God", or one that sees it as an established institution of hierarchical and sacramental mediation. To sacrifice that dimension would be to betray the *raison d'être* of ecclesial existence. Vatican II made it abundantly clear that the Church must abandon its counter positions and join in the quest of modern man for human brotherhood upon a livable earth. It supported action to achieve those ends and established as its only norm that "it should harmonize with the genuine good of the human race, and allow men as individuals and as members of society to pursue their total vocation and fulfil it". It conceded the "autonomy of earthly affairs", stating that societies have autonomous ends of their own. It accepted the independence of science, providing only that it adhere to moral norms.[11] But it also emphasized that "earthly progress must be carefully distinguished from the growth of Christ's kingdom".[12] The call of *Gaudium et Spes* is to abandon the counter-positions, to shed the semi-integralism that disfigured the Catholic stance in the previous period, but it is not a call to abandon that healthy unadjustment that is essential to the Church's relation to the world. Indeed, it reminded the Church that the "Apostles' warning" still stood: "Be not conformed to this world" (Rom. 12. 2).[13]

We have not really gone beyond Saint Augustine: "Accordingly, two cities have been formed by two loves: the earthly by the love of self, even to the contempt of God; the heavenly by the love of God, even to the contempt of self." One seeks "glory from men" but the other's glory is God, "the witness of conscience". The earthly city has its "good in this world", but it is not a good "which can discharge its devotees of all distress", and therefore "this city is often divided against itself by litigations, wars, quarrels, and such victories as are either life-destroying or short-lived". In so far as it protects peace and justice, the earthly city fulfils God's will, but its peace is an "earthly peace", while that of the city of God is "connected with eternal peace". These "two cities are commingled", and although God's judgment is always present it cannot be discerned.[14]

To the aims of the city of man to preserve peace and justice, modern technology adds another—the utilization of the earth's resources for human welfare. *Gaudium et Spes* emphasized this, and took a more optimistic position generally. Yet the lines drawn by Augustine represent the perennial Catholic position.

[11] *Ibid.*, arts. 35 and 36.
[12] *Ibid.*, art. 39.
[13] *Ibid.*, art. 37.
[14] Saint Augustine, *City of God*, Book 14, ch. 28; Book 15, ch. 4; Book 10, ch. 14; Book 19, ch. 26; Book 20, ch. 1.

The vocation of the city of man is seen in terms of the second and third foci we have delineated above; that of the Church with the fourth. The city of man so conceived is not simply the "earthly city", nor is the Church simply the city of God. And the love of self infects both. Yet the relation between the second and third foci and the fourth focus is one of tension and to some extent rivalry. The Church and the institutions that embody the second and third foci stand in two forms of tension. In so far as they tend to stand respectively for the two cities they are opponents; in so far as they represent their respective foci, and therefore justifiable parts of man's total vocation, they are in tension and to some extent in competition. They are both communities of vocation that call to men in depth. When either of them is pursued professionally, mixed motivation enters in. As a consequence the two cities are commingled here below. The Christian layman faces the difficult task of putting together membership in, and responsibility to, the two communities of vocation. The Church faces the problem of proclaiming its own superior call, while at the same time giving valence to the worth of the earthly vocation. The Church long tried to reconcile the antinomies involved by setting up an abstract architectonic hierarchy of ends, which—while it provided general guide-lines—did not make easy the anguished decisions involved.[15]

The Church as the institutional embodiment of the call to one vocation—not necessarily of the vocation itself—and the society as that of the other remain ever in a state of reciprocal tension. Positive management of this tension is one that enables the Church to be of service to the layman in putting together his two vocations, and that enables the Church itself to relate its own values which derive from its fundamental religious experience to the needs of its contemporary societal setting. Positive management of that inevitable tension does not mean abandoning the city of God under the pressure of contemporary sociological conditioning, as it too often meant in the past abandoning the city of man under the impact of the sociological conditioning of the time. For the Church to serve society and the total vocation of modern man, it must remain true to its own call—to be a sacrament, a sign and an instrument, of the relationship to which

[15] For example, see Saint Thomas, *Summa Contra Gentiles*.

the world-transcendent God calls men.[16] God and man, world and society, constitute the abiding quarternary structure within which the human drama is enacted—both the drama whose basic theme is "subdue the earth" and "replenish it" (Gen. 1. 28) and that whose theme is the call to "become the sons of God" (Jn. 1. 12). The four foci we have delineated represent four legitimate aspects of man's condition and his calling. To relate them together in a way that gives the Christian calling its proper position and yet relates it meaningfully to the earthly calling is the perennial problem of the Christian layman. To aid the layman meet that problem and to proclaim the Christian call to the world, while interpreting its implications for the life of man here below remains the task of the Church.

All acted-out answers to the great constitutive question, What ought man to be doing? inhibit some aspects of man—including aspects quite worthy of expression. The Christian answer varies in specific content in different situations, but it always tends to overshadow the other vocation. Too often in the past its one-sided understanding has made the inhibitions it involved appear as an offence.

V. THE PROBLEM OF FAITH AND CULTURE

The Church began as something like a sect, withdrawn and reserved with respect to the world. It developed into a Church that entered the world to convert it, itself inevitably to be tainted by the world's slow stain.[17] Moreover, it created about itself a Christian culture, and in the Middle Ages a Christian civilizational order. Although it often found itself in conflict with elements of that order, it nevertheless found in it a protective shield. The Church lived in a milieu that drew its basic premises from Catholicism and a culture that acted both as propadeutic and support for the act and habit of faith. Seen from the sociological point of view, the Church rests finally and essentially upon this psychological act. In human terms, faith is indeed a frail base upon which to erect so vast an edifice: "Now faith is the substance of things hoped for, the evidence of things not seen" (Heb

[16] De ecclesia, art. 1.

[17] See Ernst Troeltsch, The Social Teaching of the Christian Churches, Vols. 1 and 11 (New York & London, 1931).

11. 1). The meaning of faith is found only in faith itself; its epistemological justification in itself alone as well: "Uncertainty is the very essence of Christianity. The feeling of security in a 'world full of gods' its lost with the gods themselves; when the world is de-divinized, communication with the world-transcendent God is reduced to the tenuous bonds of faith, in the sense of Heb. 11: ... The bond is tenuous indeed and may snap easily."[18] As Saint Thomas put it, faith is "less certain" than knowledge "because matters of faith are above the human intellect".[19] Human societies rest upon the unstable basis of premisses that cannot be proven rationally or empirically. They rest in part upon positive human dispositions, as faith involves both intellect and will. They claim to derive their final legitimation from the Beyond, and their stability rests upon their members' attitude towards the Beyond. This frail basis is supplemented by consensually validated custom which provides a supportive credibility structure.

In the Christian case the difficulty is increased. Although the biblical breakthrough made known to man a call to relationship with God which dwarfed by comparison all other human vocations, it did so in a way subject to all the limitations to which our flesh is heir. It is a vision to be held on to only by faith, and faith is tenuous amidst the vicissitudes of life.[20] Hence Christian institutions are more liable to be undermined by doubt. In the Christian ages, the Church supplemented the tenuousness of faith with a Catholic civilizational order. It did something similar during the modern period by maintaining a "neo-sectarian" stance and holding to the counter-positions, but such defence proved difficult and disfiguring. In all this it tried not only to defend the substance of faith but to preserve the cultural context in which faith would be supported and protected. Increasing pluralism more and more undermined the former credibility structure. Today faith stands exposed to the neutral and hostile environments of a pluralistic and changing world.

How should the Church meet this situation? Should it develop

---

[18] Eric Voegelin, *The New Science of Politics* (Chicago, Ill., 1952), p. 122.
[19] *Summa Theologica*, IIa IIae, Ques. 4, art. 8.
[20] Here I speak as a sociologist. For the theological aspects of this problem, see Saint Thomas, *Summa Theologica*, IIa IIae, Ques. 8.

a sectarian stance and attempt to create its own cultural enclave? Can that be any longer done? Or should it experiment with new forms of religious life in order to evolve functional equivalents of forms that worked in the past? That would mean developing various forms of *ecclesiola in ecclesia* that might be functionally equivalent to the monasteries in the early Middle Ages. Indeed, are we recognizing how significant the role of the monasteries could be today? Do not the times call for a new Cluny? It appears that, though the viable solutions for the twenty-first century are not visible to us now, they will be unlike what we have called either church or sect in the past, and yet that they must incorporate elements of both.

VI. "Moulting"

We live in the great moulting period of the world, and this moulting is taking place with the Church as well. This kind of situation has existed before but it always issued in either the failure to moult and the consequent stagnation of civilizations, or in their breakdown. The Church lived before in a society whose moulting led to breakdown, and survived it to preside over the birth of a new civilization. Can it manage the present crisis, now world-wide and characterized by unprecedented dynamisms?

Catholics too long refused to face the implications of moulting. They refused to face the meaning of what Tillich called the "Protestant principle". No human institution can successfully wholly embody the relation to ultimacy. Social forms come into existence, change, and pass out of existence. Now they have recognized these things. Yet now they face the danger of substituting for their former over-absolutization of historically specific forms an equally spurious over-relativization that loses its grip upon timeless essentials. Their long years of self-segregation render them naïve in their new contact with a dynamic pluralistic world and make them susceptible to such temptations. The modern world has not solved its own profound crisis. Protestantism has certainly not developed impressive answers to the problems we have discussed here. While Catholics have much to learn from both secular modern man and from the Protestant experience, it is not there that they will find solutions to this most important complex of questions. Catholics must engage in dialogue and co-operation with others but they must retain a keen sense of the Catholic problem. The vertical dimension is a relation to Transcendence, but its institutional embodiment remains ever relative. Both aspects must be firmly grasped.

Moreover, every answer to the constitutive question neglects and represses elements of the human potential—and often elements worthy of expression. Every vocation is at the same time a discipline. In a time of moulting, when the society is shedding the forms of its older answer to the constitutive question, What ought man to be doing?, what had been neglected finds new avenues of expression and what had been repressed returns. Hence what we called above the first focus becomes a significant element in the situation. That is palpably the case in today's world. Yet, as every psychoanalyst knows all too well, the return of the repressed is not only upsetting, it is often of a mixed character. Uncritical acceptance of impulse in such a setting would be unwise indeed. What returns contains elements that can enrich and broaden our self-realization and deepen our culture, but it also contains elements whose uncritical acceptance would lead to the social equivalent of a neurotic acting-out of repressed impulses.

Emerging out of a situation of fixity of forms and of constraint, Catholics are now subject to the kind of swing from one extreme to another so characteristic of human affairs, and are in serious need to guard against it. The cross is still the symbol of Christianity; the pendulum cannot be substituted for it.

Stephan Pfürtner

Pathology of the Catholic Church

THE term "pathology" derives from medicine. Its use in the present context is not without dangers. The Church is not a physical body. Nevertheless, since St Paul, it has been compared to a body. Therefore associated figures seem justifiable. But is this the time to begin a "scientific examination of the sickness" that affects this churchly body and its organs? Many are disturbed by such an attempt; others think that the many similar efforts being made today are destructive. Medicine treats pathology as an essential prerequisite in its service to the health of mankind. Should it be any different in the case of the Church?

In the attempts to elucidate the causes of the diseased nature of church life today, two opposed views constantly recur: one asserts that the lack of religious and ecclesiastical spirit, the degeneration of belief and moral energy, the secularization of thought, and so on, are at fault. It therefore calls for a moral or religious renewal of all branches of the Church, and above all, of course, of church people. The other viewpoint opines that an interpretation of the foregoing kind serves only to conceal the real causes, which are to be sought elsewhere: in, that is, outdated church structures. The debate about the state of the priesthood, which was carried on in connection with the Roman Synod of 1971, emphasized these positions. The European priest delegates in Geneva brought the second viewpoint forward, and made the Church aware of it on an international level. It is possible that socio-historical experiences outside the Church have really made us alive to the issue: theological grounds alone do

not enable us to examine the problem of whether there are structures in the Church (possibly in terms of the personal integrity
of their office-holders) which contradict the nature of the Church
and its mission (as conceived in evangelical terms) for today's
world. Why is this?

I. A Criticism of Structures demanded by the Gospel

"Christ summons the Church, as she goes her pilgrim way, to
that continual reformation of which she always has need, in so
far as she is an institution of men here on earth" (Vatican II:
Ecumenism, 6). Here the Vatican Council formulated a principle whose implications—as so often with important conciliar
statements—are of an importance that has hardly as yet been
proficiently appreciated, at least to the extent that they are taken
quite seriously. In the present context, it means that *no* existing
church structure is withdrawn from reform in the light of the
experientially believed Gospel, and may be presented as enjoying
divine sanction pure and simple. For, in so far as a structure
exists in the conditions of actuality, and therefore in the order of
facticity, it is also (in any form it may take) "of men here on
earth". Hence it necessarily remains behind the full demands
of the Gospel. The criticism of structures is a theological postu-
late.

Of course, attacks on social structures in the Church are no
less explosive than in the secular or political world. For in the
case of social structures we are always faced with an institutionalization of the distribution of power and the exertion of
power. It is a matter of claims to "mandatory power" over the led
claimed by the leaders. It is a matter of the freedoms and rights
of the leaders and of the restrictions of freedom and power of
the led—in the name of existing orders, or by means of a false
appeal to them. Therefore it is understandable that the debate
should be so emotively conceived.

Obviously, responsible structural criticism cannot treat of the
removal of all structures. The decisive question is rather what
form of institutionalized distribution of power can justifiably
exist. The social consciousness of our times no longer permits us
to characterize actual conditions purely and simply as the best, let

alone as absolutely valid. Nowadays we know to what extent an unjustifiable and illegal will to power lay behind the assertions of sun kings or other monarchs that their claim to rule was grounded in "divine right". The experiences of our societal and institutional history show that wherever power is exercised over men and this exercise of power is stabilized, the danger of its misuse enters in. Under the defence of legitimately existent mandates, forms of domination have constantly established themselves which for the dominated meant repression and the maintenance of injustice. Theologically, this might be expressed as the inborn will to power that is part of original sin.

Had the holders of power in the Church really the right to represent themselves as unassailable in this regard? Of course defenders of the existing conditions of office and power do not contest that there *was* a misuse of power in the Church. But they attribute it to the sinful weakness of individuals, and refuse to derive it from the ecclesiastical structures—since they are possessed of a "divine right". But how do things look when the existing structures of the Church, which perhaps enjoyed some reasonable justification in the past, have become in the meantime ways of access to the misuse of power, or even expressions of institutionalized domination? Can the corresponding structures then really still base themselves on "divine right"? Here, to dominate men means to deprive men of their basic rights to freedom and self-determination, as these rights have in the meantime asserted themselves and been recognized historically in our moral consciousness, and thus to rob them of their human dignity. To exercise domination of this kind is to do injustice. Should ecclesiastical structures be shown to have functions of this kind, then, whether convenient or not, they must be exposed as ideological partisan positions serving to defend unjust power privileges.

II. HUMAN RIGHTS—THE DECISIVE CRITERION

Is there an institutionalized misuse of power in the Church? All church reform must be oriented by the answer to this question. Respect for basic human rights should be the criterion for the theological quest for truth that we undertake here. For human rights afford us something obviously valid, injury to which is incontestably injustice. Of course it cannot be denied that there are systems in the Church which are founded upon divine right. Yet their actual interpretation is a matter of social history and far too easily falls victim to ideological claims. All religious office holders, even those of Christianity, have in the course of human history raised claims upon the basis of the authority given them by their office, which were later shown to be inimical to religion. Hence the difficult task of reaching judgment in this context requires yardsticks whose validity is incontestable.

Of course, recourse to fundamental rights does not mean an advocacy of utopian demands for man. It is just as little a matter of a radical equalization of all areas of competence in the Church. There is no society which is able to ensure its members all possible liberties and rights. In human society there will always be tension between the desire for possible greater freedoms and the rights for every man that are actually achieved. Equality of rights must certainly form the critical last line of defence against all unjustified commerce in privileges. But, since Aristotle's thoughts on right in the ordered city state, our socio-philosophical tradition has recognized the necessity of acknowledging a proportional equality of rights for all: with "to each his own" as the basic axiom. Even the most radical socialist communes finally have to admit that "to each the same" is not enough.

Nevertheless there are rights which civilized nations would accord to all men in the same way. The Church has long fundamentally acknowledged these rights. Yet it has not formed its own structures in accordance with the newly developed understanding of the individual and of right. Hence the Church is in a state of self-conflict. It is torn between, on the one hand, the understanding of authority derived from classical antiquity, the Middle Ages and feudal times, and, on the other, the history of freedom in the modern age. The following are a few examples of impaired fundamental rights, which may stand for others and which are symptomatic of whole areas.

III. The Natural Right to Marriage

It is generally acknowledged that marriage is an elementary human right. A man has to decide whether he will marry—

though, of course, while considering the rights of others who might be affected by his action. In actuality, it is evident that the authorities of the Church often make extensive inroads on this fundamental right. One example is the regulations and dispensations for partners of different churches and faiths. Another is the practice of ecclesiastical marriage law. In this area the law of the Church has been, and is, far too often put above the natural basic right of man, and the competence of clerics placed above the individual's right of self-determination. This is experienced as an intolerable form of compulsion in countries where the civil and ecclesiastical forms of marriage are not yet separate, and non-Catholics or Catholics alienated from the Church are nevertheless subject to the code. Here is a decisive symptom of theocracy still being exercised in our own times, whereby, on grounds of religious ideology, men claim the power of judgment over the basic social rights of other men. The conditions and circumstances brought about by the law of celibacy also belong in this context. What does it really mean when the Pope and a good number of bishops, without any adequate consultation of their priests and without their co-operation in the formation of opinion, authoritatively declare that compulsory celibacy must continue in the Church? They imagine that their office gives them this right. But here the claim of office is set against a basic human right. The priest denied himself marriage before his ordination. The right to do that, however, is so very much a part of the elementary context of human self-disposition, that respect for him demands that he should thereafter be primarily considered in all decisive processes which have to do with this right. Are we really to believe that because they once gave their consent to celibacy, at the time of their ordination, for the rest of their lives priests are to be deprived of fundamental right in this area? Ossified structures are allowed to decide the fates of innumerable human beings. It is no longer a secret that at least a part of the clergy can no longer—for a variety of reasons—accept compulsory celibacy. Have a few men, such as the Pope and bishops, really the right to dispose of the lives of thousands of other men, even against the convinced consciences of those men? What *is a man* in the Church?

The assertion that the priests in question are free to give up their priesthood if they really want to get married, is very questionable. It not only shows how negatively church thinking still conceives marriage and sex (clearly, the acceptance of a life of faith and the readiness of many to devote their existence henceforth to the service of the Church and the world do not outweigh their "worthless" decision in regard to marriage), but denies the fact that vocational and economic existence for most is bound up with their office. This leads to certain pressures which prevent many from surrendering their office. Many priests and religious do not have any sickness or old age insurance. It is fundamentally questionable whether under these circumstances a religious profession can still be exercised in a state of genuine religious freedom. It is clear, too, that another basic right is affected in this regard—that of "religious liberty". The actualization of this right is still missing in many contexts within the Catholic Church; unfortunately there is not space enough to pursue them here.

IV. The Right to search for Truth

This is another right which is endangered in the Church. It includes the freedom of doctrine and research in theology and the right to publish and express one's opinion freely. Here too the Council made a basic assertion: "By reason of their nature as social beings all men explain to one another the truth they have discovered, or think they have discovered, in order thus to assist one another in the quest for truth" (*Declaration on Religious Freedom*, 3). But how is this principle adhered to within the Church itself? Of course, in the meantime, many heartening things have occurred in this area. Nevertheless, theology professors who critically opposed *Humanae Vitae* were deprived of their teaching posts in countries where the State (as in Italy or the U.S.A.) did not accord them adequate legal protection. Heavy pressures were brought to bear on others. The journal *Il Regno* in Bologna was suppressed and its editors dismissed for writing in terms that did not accord with Roman ecclesiology. Catholic news agencies, newspapers and publishers who publish anything allegedly dangerous to the Church are put under quite massive economic pressure. The imprimatur for theological books is still required in a modified form.

All these phenomena show unmistakably that the ecclesiastical hierarchy claims the competence to restrict or, if necessary, to make of no effect the social right of others to search for truth within the Church. It should not be forgotten that, considered sociologically like any trade union or political party, the Church is a partisan organization, of the kind that gives personalities which accord with its dominant ideas a dominant influence. But there are not only parties but churches which allow their members the basic right to co-operate actively in the development of the best form of self-understanding, in the search for truth, and in the evolution of will and purpose in their particular community, and which have therefore mastered the problem of doctrinal order without affecting the basic right to freedom of doctrine and research, and the free expression of opinion.

V. The Church—A Religious Class Society

This brings us to one of the most pressing tasks of Catholic structural reform for coming generations. Sociologically, a class society exists where a social stratum lays claim to rights which it fundamentally denies others. Privileges result in their holders being the determinative and active subjects (in the specific area of right) and the others the determined and acted-upon objects. The latter can participate in the power of those who exercise power by grace and favour: they can be their helpers and instruments, but never enjoy any specific rights of their own in the process, or any *status activus*. In religio-historical terms, the sacred class society is especially manifest in religions with a caste system.

It cannot be denied that the Catholic Church contains important effective elements of a religious class society. More detailed religio-sociological findings must await more extensive research. Here it is possible only to indicate known complexes in a general way. Whoever knows anything about life in the Church is aware of the barriers that still exist between the laity and the clergy, despite all glorification of the laity. When decisive ecclesiastical positions are in question, laymen just do not come into question in far too many cases. The isolation of the clergy and religious throughout their education, and a corresponding consciousness, are still effective in many individuals, right down to the smallest detail of the effective contexts within which they encounter the laity. The exceptions, where real loyalty and team work on a basis of equal rights do obtain, as, say, in the Netherlands, are still rare. Whenever laymen attain to important offices in church affairs, attempts are made to appoint "spiritual directors" for them in some kind of way. At any rate, this certainly happens in several hospitals and educational establishments in Federal Germany. And of course there is the continuing class stratification within the clergy itself. The Pope enjoys other rights than the bishops, who in their turn have rights other than those of their "lower clergy".

In classification in this field it is not a question only of something awry in the present circumstances, but much more of fundamental (allegedly dogmatically grounded) church structures which profoundly determine the constitution of the Catholic Church. The laity and the lower clergy are constitutionally excluded from decision processes in the Church. They are allowed to participate in it only in so far as the episcopate permits. They cannot lay any claim to further participation. Only the bishops in union with the Pope possess the rights of decision and leadership. In ecclesiastical jargon, this is called the power of teaching and jurisdiction: "This power . . . is proper, ordinary and immediate" (*Dogmatic Constitution on the Church*, 27). Vatican II proved unable to change anything in this respect.

VI. No Division or Control of Power

Experiences of the misuse of power led secular society over the centuries to distribute the functions of power and to establish various forms of power control (parliament for government, a free press, and so forth). In this respect we are only at the beginning in the Catholic Church. The people have not achieved a distribution of power, or any other form of control of power. The legislative, judiciary and executive are the cumulative possession of the upper ranks of the hierarchy. The lower clergy and the laity (to say nothing of women as such) enjoy an inferior form of constitutional right. If their representatives come into conflict with the other stratum, they are essentially disadvantaged

by the structures. The representatives of the hierarchy determine what is right and truth. It is only to be expected that
they should try to confirm their rights. They for the most part
also have the economic power in the Church. The Catholic
Church has often fought against any form of discrimination between men because of race, social level, or religion. However, the
upper levels of the Church will not admit that it is itself—in
sociological terms—a class society. In it, an upper stratum lays
claim to competence in the realm of active rights which is alleged
to extend even to the basic human rights. The derivation of this
claim from tradition is well known.

That the constitution of the New Testament communities can
in no way be identified with the hierarchical structure of the
Catholic Church no longer needs any demonstration. The undifferentiated citation of individual biblical texts to support hierarchical claims and the "estates" within the Church must
therefore, in the light of New Testament hermeneutics, be judged
unjustifiable, and—for professional theologians—irresponsible.
The assertion of essentially different estates and rights in the
Church approximates so closely to arguments which were at one
time used to defend monarchy and feudal domination that for
this reason alone great critical acuity is necessary in this area.
The assertion that "God's grace" has been granted one because
"all power is from above", and that truth is non-elective, and so
on, is the axiom of all absolutist thought. The corollary of such
argumentation is that the people are unfit to govern themselves
because they are too stupid, or because individuals are too egotis-
tic (W. Strelewicz). In ecclesiastical jargon this is expressed not
so much directly as through well-known biblical images of, say,
the sheep who have need of the shepherds ordained by God. Perhaps (!) this originated in an age when "the people" were largely
illiterate—to be able to read and write was in the first centuries
of church history a rare privilege of the top cultural strata, and
for the most part even of the clergy. Is that true today?

In any case all synods and councils have treated "the truth" as
elective. Every pope in recent epochs has been entrusted with his
competence—relative to his office—"from below", by, that is,
the cardinals. And the prime minister of a modern democracy
must not understand his commission and his powers as being any

less an office from God than a monarch of earlier times. On this basis, therefore, there can be no foundation for our church structures. Such a basis must be sought in the context of social history. But its component factors are usually treated quite uncritically in hierarchical circles.

It is not insignificant that Paul VI spoke of the constitution of the Church as essentially "hierarchical and monarchical" (address of 21.11.64: *Act. Apost. Sed.*, 56 (1964), 1012), and emphasized that as far as rights within it are concerned it is constitutively *societas inaequalis*—an unequal society (*Act. Apost. Sed.*, 57 (1965), 985), unequal in terms of competences and rights. Is it also unequal in respect for human dignity?

VII. The Gospel—The End of the Epiphany Religions

There are certainly men of different levels of "dignity" in the Catholic Church. Of course, in the meantime there have been attempts to express such things differently. "Eminences", "Excellencies" and "Monsignori" are not recommended terms. This is a happy sign of a new awareness of solidarity which is also affirmed and sought for by many bishops. But in the long run such things must be socially ineffective if the institutions themselves remain unaltered. These tend to have a self-revivifying effect. So long as they are there, they tend like ruts in a roadway to keep back the wheels of the social vehicle. Luther's outspokenness against hierarchical dignities and the personality cult has clearly not had much effect in the area of rights and social criticism within the Catholic Church. The reformer asserted that all were equal in *dignitas humana*, in human dignity. The Enlightenment, the French Revolution and the Socialist movements extended this basic idea—often murderously. But does that mean that the idea itself has lost its validity? Indeed, it should be counted among the essential contents of the Bible and the history of its action. To be a human being is our proper and uniquely inalienable dignity; it is the highest title of nobility granted us by God.

This means that no one has any basic right to diminish another's dignity: neither the Christian in regard to non-Christians, nor the "ordained" in regard to those without "ordination". We are all no more than human beings, equal in the extent of our human dignity, equal in the poverty of our creaturely weakness and nakedness. The variation in education, estate and origin, in office, service and responsibility, should not be denied or levelled-down, in society or in the Church. It must correspond to a differentiation of acknowledgment and responsibility. But all this concerns the level of service and functions, and not that of the humanness of the appropriate dignity and fundamental rights. What, in contradistinction to that, do all human titles mean? Every man is an "equal image" of the highest, every one is "another Christ", essentially confirmed in his importance and freedom. The modern consciousness of autonomy, individuality and rights of man does not contradict the Gospel, and might even be said to express its essential proclamation better than earlier times. It should really be seen as containing far less that is dangerous than the ecclesiastical "anti-Modernists" of the last and this century though it featured in terms of "rationalism", "laicism" or unbelief.

No less dangerous for Christian life in faith are those ideas, value categories and forms of behaviour which belong to the history of religions—to paganism—and which have undeniably entered into our church structures. What is really happening to Catholics when they encounter the People high above the ordinary people in St Peter's Square, blessing them from his Vatican window? "The representative of Christ—Christ on earth", said a man standing next to me, and looked up with tears in his eyes as if he were watching an epiphany of Christ. In the Mediterranean area the faithful still kiss the hand of a passing priest, and bow down as if there were some kind of manifestation of the divine in the "ordained" man—even though they themselves are baptized in God's Holy Spirit. Of course there are spontaneous relations here with archaic tribal religions and their numinous adoration of the possessors of power, or with Roman and East Asian emperor cults. The history of religion is full of these phenomena, which extend to every continent. The ancient Egyptians supposed that their god-king was the incarnation or the epiphany of their god—as did the ancient Peruvians. The constitution of the cult in the Roman Catholic Church with "higher office-holders" does little "on theological grounds" to prevent such associations. We are led to recall not only the ancient ordination and sacramental theology according to which the priest and above all the bishop received "an indelible seal" with their ordination, becoming sacramentally or "ontologically" different from their previous state, other than the "simple laity" and therefore special manifestations of the divine. (Just think of the cultic halo that surrounds a new priest at his first mass!) We must also consider the latest standpoints in ecclesiology. Since Pius XII, it is asserted that the bishops, and of course the Pope, should be granted a special kind of religious respect in their directions to the faithful (*Dogmatic Constitution on the Church*, 25). Not only the "ministry" of "service" to the Church and the world would distinguish the bishop from other men, but "something is to be inserted between Christ and the community of the faithful which separates (*separet*) them", that is, their membership of the hierarchy. Anyone who denies the difference is alleged to contradict the message of the Gospel, according to Paul VI (address of 20.11.1965; *Act. Apost. Sed.*, 57 (1965), 985), What does this mean in realistic terms if not that the Pope and the bishops are "special beings", different in their existence and its fundamental conditions to ordinary mortal men, i.e., beings in whom God is present in a special way?

The eccentricities possible on this basis are shown in the case of Archbishop Benelli. He seriously asserts that in the exercise of his office the Pope is not subject to any restrictions imposed by human ageing. Christ assured Peter of his support "in spite of, and beyond, the years, infirmity and sickness" (cited according to the *Kirchenzeitung für d. Erzbistum Köln* of 24 September 1971, p. 2). If only such pundits would remember even Aquinas's principle that grace presupposes nature. And what would they say if a pope happened to fall victim to a brain tumour, advanced cancer of another kind, or a chronic sclerosis, with all the accompanying symptoms of personality change known to modern medicine? Benelli's assertion shows to what extremes of denial of reality imprisonment in a religious ideology can lead one. And surely he must have remembered the advance signs of the mortal infirmities of John XXIII or Pius XII. The Gospel certainly cannot be quoted as an authoritative source for such ideas, which can be elucidated only in terms of the latent effect of mythic ideas, say that of the messengers of the gods, that has come to us from antiquity, or other religio-historical schemata.

VIII. DEMYTHOLOGIZATION OF THE HIERARCHY

Here we have reached the core of this complex of problems. It is clear that all reform of structures and human rights in the Church is ultimately a theological problem. It is not today (as at one time in the Reformation) primarily a matter of the removal of moral misunderstandings. It is a question of God and the acknowledgment of his incomparable and inalienable majesty. In our times that acknowledgment is joined with the claim that human dignity and the consequent basic human rights are to be recognized as inalienable. The New Testament faith in God radically forbids the replacement of God with any creature of God. Just as fundamentally it forbids any replacement of the only mediator, Christ, with anyone else characterized as a wholly competent divine mediator. Every form of deification (divinization) of any man is unbelief. God is God. Man is and remains man. The Pope and the bishops, like all of us, are merely men, however great their service to the Church may be. Therefore we in the Church must return to that simplicity—the true form of humility—which is demanded by theological faith and factually relevant realism. Belief in the Church and the divine proclamation regarding it must be reconstituted on this basis. We do not believe in the Church by virtue of an historical integrity which it does not possess. To assert that would be to revert to the *theologica gloriae*. We believe in it by virtue of the promise of God that, with his Spirit and his word, he would always maintain truth in it. There should be no secret or even open identification of God and his Church, of the word of its office-holders and the word of God, of the Pope and Christ: not even on the level of the "infallibility" of the magisterium. Such an equation must be judged theologically inadmissible. Therefore, theologically responsible discourse should expose the erroneous interpretation of such titles as "representative of Christ", *"Summus Pontifex"*, and so on. There must be a corresponding clear rejection of the claim that any ecclesiastical office-holders have, by virtue of their hierarchical dignity, any "divine" competence over men in terms of their basic human rights. Anything to the contrary must be characterized as a (conscious or unconscious) attempt to alienate man from himself and to subject him to a theocratic form of domination, which is certainly the most sublime form of all domination.

But what remains for the "mass" of religious men when the "representatives" of God on earth have been demythologized and declared to be ordinary men? Where are the countless men who required some tangible, visible support to ground their faith? This is no new question. In our own times it was perhaps put most acutely by Dostoevsky in the figure of the "Grand Inquisitor". The right answer can only come from the New Testament. It leads to the core of faithful existence, as interpreted, for instance, by the Pauline writings. Faith lives from what is not visible, as the "assurance of things hoped for, the conviction of things not seen" (Heb. 11. 1). Therefore "we look not to the things that are seen but to the things that are unseen" (2 Cor. 4. 18). Faith does not live from the appearance—the epiphany of the divine in any miracles and powers, men or cults. Theological faith lives from God, the concealed, the intangible. The task of ecclesiastical office-holders cannot be to understand and present themselves as the proper reference-points for the people. They do not visibly represent the invisible as a kind of reincarnation of the divine. Every office in the Church is no more—and of course no less—than service in the construction of the Church and the world. Fraternal service in the office of a bishop means being of assistance to everyone in terms of the faith of the Gospel, instead of tying it down to pseudo-theological categories of a religio-historical kind. Only a faith of this kind makes men free; nly that kind of faith is worthy of God and of the Church and of man. Any other form of faith involves religious compulsions, even when at first it seems emotionally gratifying.

Anyone who asserts that the "mass" of religious men are not capable of this kind of "naked faith" not only thereby expresses his contempt for the ordinary man, but claims to be able to offer him something better or easier than God does in the Gospel. We find salvation only in the light of the cross. Correspondingly, faith lives from that which is unseen. Jesus of Nazareth was deprived in his death of all visible and tangible evidences of his acceptance by God. In this way—and not by way of security in the visible—he was able to become the "loyal and true witness" of God and his holy action upon us. Whenever theological faith strives to become existentially relevant, everyone must experience the same destiny. It must undertake the destruction of all signs of power so as to acknowledge no grounds other than God himself and his promise, which surpasses all comprehension. Is this way too difficult for us men? Is the way abroad demanded too extreme and too radical? In this process, the Church can and must help us by repeatedly affording us the word of promise, and by mediating the experience of our fellow travellers. It never can, and never should, put itself in the place of God, on any pretext whatsoever.

Translated by John Griffiths

Yves Congar

Renewal of the Spirit and Reform of the Institution

"INSTITUTION" is not a very precise term and is open to a number of definitions. It is derived from the Latin *instituere, statuere, stare*, and from the Greek *istêmi*, meaning to establish or erect. It usually designates a certain structure of a relatively permanent nature which is the product of a superior will (not simply of nature) and answers an aim or a need, and in which individuals find a model for their behaviour and an indication of their group role. The apostolate, the Church and the sacraments are institutions proceeding from a divine institutional will, but their historical forms—that is, their structures—were the work of human interventions.

The religious orders, the demarcation of dioceses, and the organization of ministries and offices, schools or hospitals, are ecclesiastical institutions. Revelation is a divine institution, but dogmatic formulas—and still more preaching, the teaching of the ordinary magisterium, dogmatic theologies and theologies proper—are its human ecclesiastical expressions.

Every society features tensions between its acquired forms, its institutions and structures, and the free movement of the spirit, since the spirit never ceases to create, and the constant advance into the unknown future of history calls for a no less constant questioning of acquired forms. This is equally true for the society which is the Church. In this case there are specific reasons in view of the fact that the Church, while being historical and man-made, is not a purely human society. This is apparent in two main ways: (1) the Church possesses a truth which it does not

39

freely bestow upon itself, but which comes to it from God: either at its origin, in the models which it has in the Old Testament, the incarnation of the suffering servant, the *ecclesia primitiva* (a constant point of reference, even though it has been idealized in all reforms), or at its ending. It does not know this end in the way in which one would be aware of a definite project, but it exists, God calls the Church to it, and it must tend towards it.

God is not only behind the Church, at its beginning; he is also before it: he calls it to prepare and to anticipate his reign. The feeling of the never bridged distance between the historical Church and its truth, that of its Alpha and that of its Omega, is the major source of all reform movements. It grounds the consciousness of historicity, and therefore that of relativity and of the forms in which the institution is realized. There is no ecclesiology which does not have to assume as a statutory fact the irreducible duality of that which exists in fact and that which ought to exist. All the descendants of Abraham are not true sons of Abraham (Rom. 9. 7), the people can be a non-people (Hos. 1. 9); several appear to be within who are in fact without (St Augustine).

(2) The Church has as its inward principle of unity and life the person of the Holy Spirit (whether by means of the category of appropriation or in some other way, this affirmation must hold). Yet it is true that the Spirit has no autonomy in relation to Christ in the work that he does (cf. Jn. 16. 13–15); but it is also true that in the realization of his work, he is grace, and therefore liberty—the Event. The event cannot be set against, or reduced to, the institution. Yet that was certainly the tendency of the dominant ecclesiology during the anti-Protestant centuries, the times of set affirmation of authority (the nineteenth century), whatever the actual life of the Church (which this ecclesiology interpreted so inadequately) may have been. I could cite many witnesses for the reduction of the Holy Spirit to the role of guarantor of the hierarchical, sacramental or magisterial institution. Yet the Spirit, according to Hans Urs von Balthasar's profound definition, is the "Unknown beyond the Word".[1] The Church does not proceed from the unique mission of the word, which

---

[1] Hans Urs von Balthasar, "Der Unbekannte jenseits des Wortes", in *Interpretation der Welt* (Würzburg, 1966), pp. 638–45.

has established in this world, at least in substantial terms, a definite form of faith, sacraments and ministry. It also proceeds from a second mission: that of the Spirit, which continually bears forward into the unknown future of history the work done once for all by Christ, and which on that account never ceases to stimulate and inspire men, while constantly bringing new life to the Church (St Irenaeus).

Since St Paul (Rom. 12. 2; Eph. 4. 23), there has always been an advocacy in the Church of a renewal of life by means of a transformation of the spirit. The theme of "reform" is so fundamental to, and coextensive with, the life of the Church that the *"Textus emendatus"* of the *Lex Ecclesiae Fundamentalis* (1971) has acknowledged it (can. 2, art. 4); initially, it was treated by the Fathers and by the liturgy as a Christian anthropological theme.[2] It was a question essentially of the reshaping of man in the likeness of God that sin made him lose. *Intus reformari* is the work in us of the saving incarnation. That is a chapter of "spirituality": that is, of life according to the Spirit, whose truth is always up to date. It is the preaching of *metanoia* and Shrovetide. To take self-reform seriously according to the standards of the Gospel and the *sequela Christi* can lead one far. Francis of Assisi did no more than this.

Yet this is not enough.

First of all, we must remember that the unconditional defenders of authority (when it was not the authority of the *status quo*) freely developed a theme which went like this: Reform yourselves and all will go well; then the most urgent problems are resolved.[3] This may also be seen as one form of a widespread tendency among Catholics (at least until their recent awakening to the meaning of the political dimensions of things, and of the conditions for any real efficacy): a tendency to see only the moral aspect of problems—or rather that part of their moral aspect

[2] See G. B. Ladner, *The Idea of Reform. Its Impact on Christian Thought and Action in the Age of the Fathers* (Cambridge, Mass., 1959; new edition, New York, 1967).

[3] Cf., as an example of this in the early nineteen hundreds, the opposition to "Reform-Katholizismus": A. M. Weiss, "Reformbestrebungen" (1905—ch. 6 of *Lebens- und Gewissensfragen der Gegenwart* (Freiburg, 1911), Vol. 2, pp. 57–66, 85–100, 118 ff., 134–45); and the pamphlet by Mgr P. W. von Keppler, *Wahre und falsche Reform* (Freiburg, 1902).

deriving from intentions and purity of intention. Yet history already had some significant lessons to offer. Some strong and pure reformist currents failed to be more effective because they stayed too much in a spiritual and private realm: the movement of the "Friends of God" in the second half of the fourteenth century, and, however powerful it was, that of the *Devotio moderna* and the Brothers of Life in Common in the latter part of the same century. A spiritual renewal, limited in the first case, and more widespread in the second, had no effective impact on institutions, from the viewpoint of the reform that was really required.

Institutions have their own weight, density and permanence. Even those of the Church depend on society as a whole. This is well known to those Christians in politically committed movements who expect a radical change in the structures of the Church to come from a social revolution. It is impossible to ignore the influence of political ideas and the social context as a whole on the conception of authority and the actual conduct of life in the Church. It was not without reason that St Leo formulated his theology of papal power in terms of *principatus*. It is obvious that the absolutist and centralistic ideas which characterized monarchical power in the sixteenth, and then in the nineteenth century (with the haunting memory, then, of an ever-looming Revolution and of an authority that *had* to be affirmed), were reflected in the ecclesiology of those times.

It is true that purely spiritual attitudes also have an impact on social structures: St Francis, in rejecting oaths and recourse to arms, challenged the social structures of his own time. The Pilgrim Fathers and other emigrants for conscience' sake helped to determine the spirit of the United States. This shows that the spiritual element does take effect. It is necessary; yet it is not sufficient. There is in fact a density proper to impersonal and collective structures which has to be reached: otherwise the most generous reformist intentions would exhaust themselves in a never-ending effort that the opposing structures, keeping their place, would condemn to remain only half-effective.

History also provides us with significant examples of reforms which were *both* spiritual and structural. Examples are: the reform of the eleventh century (the "Gregorian" reform), that of the mendicant orders in the thirteenth century, that brought about by the Council of Trent, and that of Vatican II.

1. It is not my task here to retrace the complex history of the reform of the eleventh century. Several aspects of it are nevertheless worthy of discussion. It began before the pontificate of Gregory VII, but it was Gregory who was its most decisive agent. Fliche has shown (the criticisms of his book seem to me to allow this general schema to remain) that it is possible to isolate two reformist projects in the eleventh century:[4] the first, which he calls "Italian" because it was promoted by Atto of Vercelli and Peter Damian, looked for a moral reform, through preaching and example, of the abuses from which the Church suffered: simony and nicolaitanism (clerical unchastity). The "Lorraine project" (Wason of Liège, Ratherius of Verona, and—above all —Humbert of Silva Candida) was more radical. Without ignoring the moral aspect, it attacked the cause. The root of all the evils was lay investiture, by which the lay powers disposed of ecclesiastical offices and treated them in a secular fashion. When he became Gregory VII, Hildebrand adopted these views. The usual effectiveness of his action results from his inspiration of a radical programme of reform of the structures and legal status of ecclesial life, by means of a simple, fervent and intransigent mysticism of the sovereignty of God, of which papal authority was the reflection and instrument.[5] Gregory VII's power depended wholly upon his spiritual conviction. The effectiveness of his reforms was linked to various economic and political expressions of this conviction: the reform of the law relating to ecclesiastical property; support for a semi-political resistance movement against the married clergy—like the Milan *Pataria*; the financial independence of the clergy which gave rise, for example, to such a canon as the following: *"ut omnis christianus procuret ad missarum sollemnia aliquid Deo offere"* (cf. Schreiber); and the elevation and expansion of the *vita apostolica*; and so forth.[6]

[4] A. Fliche, *Le Réforme grégorienne: I. La formation des idées grégoriennes. II. Gregoire VII* (Louvain, 1924–25).

[5] This mysticism and theonomic vision without any compromise has been competently analysed by A. Nitschke, "Die Wirksamkeit Gottes in der Welt Gregors VII", *Studi Gregoriani* 5 (Rome, 1956), pp. 115–219.

[6] On this aspect of the Gregorian reform, see D. B. Zema, "Reform Legislation in the Eleventh Century and its Economic Import", *Catholic*

2. The reform introduced by St Francis and St Dominic was, originally, purely spiritual: in the case of Francis, being a conversion to the practice of the Gospel *"sine glossa"*, poverty was the condition for an evangelical attitude of absolute dependence with regard to God the Father and of absolute brotherhood with God's creatures; in the case of Dominic, the reform was the consistent practice of an apostolic charity vowed to the doctrinal service of mankind, with mendicant poverty and an organization of fraternal communities for prayer and study. These two designs were fairly diverse at the start and came to approximate one another; they had considerably revolutionary consequences in regard to the structures both of society as a whole and of ecclesiastical service.[7] They broke with the territorial and all but fixed nature of the structures produced by the feudal system; they supported the communal movement of solidarity of citizens freed from subjection to church or temporal lords. They proved so adaptable to a process of urbanization that medievalists have suggested that the "town" of the Middle Ages should be defined in terms of the establishment of a mendicant house;[8] they endowed the Word with a sort of dynamic independence, and opened the way for new missionary initiatives, detached from any context of conquest or crusade. Finally, the condition of poverty enjoined upon the mendicants allowed Jean de Paris (1302) to distinguish the Church from induced hierocratic pretensions when he made his distinction between Christ as God, who possesses the kingdom of the world, and Christ in his

---

Historical Review, 27 (1941), pp. 1 f.; "Economic Reorganization of the Roman See during the Gregorian Reform", *Studi Gregoriani*, 1 (Rome, 1947), pp. 137–681; G. Schreiber, *Gemeinschaften des Mittelalters* (Münster, 1948), pp. 370–2; Ch. Dereine, "Vie commune, Règle de S. Augustin et chanoines reguliers au XIe siécle", *Rev. Hist. eccles.*, 41 (1946), pp. 365–406.

[7] See M. D. Chenu, "Réformes de structure en Chrétienté", *Economie et Humanisme* (1946), pp. 85–98. In an article in *Archives d'Hist. doctr. et littér. du Moyen Age*, 28 (1961), pp. 35–152, I have demonstrated how in the quarrel between the seculars and the mendicants two conceptions of pastoral mission and the Church were set one against the other—one fixed and territorial, the other missionary and universalist.

[8] Results obtained by a research group under the direction of Professor J. Le Goff: cf. *Annales*, 23 (1968), pp. 335–52; 25 (1970), p. 924 f.; *Rev. Hist. Droit* (1970), pp. 390–407.

humanity, who has chosen poverty. If Jean de Paris was able to approximate to the principles posited by Thomas Aquinas in favour of an appropriate distinction between the spiritual and temporal realms, it was the system inaugurated by St Dominic which freed them both from the temporal burdens of the feudal Church.

3. John XXIII more than once described the aim of the Second Vatican Council as, optimally, both a renewal of the pastoral structures of the Church (the emphasis was often put, at first, on the revision of canon law), and a renewal—an increase—of faith and Christian life.[9] He also often stated the spiritual conditions necessary on the way towards such a process. In connecting the spiritual renewal of Christians with the canonical and pastoral reform assigned as the goal of the Council, John XXIII returned to the ancient tradition for which a reform was primarily a spiritual re-formation of the Christian individual.

How have things gone? The Council would seem to have done remarkably well in realizing its programme. God granted his Church a great access of grace on the eve of a deep-reaching, world-wide and rapid process of cultural transformation. It is very difficult to speak of the post-conciliar period proper. It presents aspects of rupture and crisis that the Council did not seem to promise. This is partly the result of the fact that a too long period of narrowness and ossification had stifled initiative: once the valves were opened, the flood was all the heavier because it had the forces of all the currents of the age behind it. Perhaps another reason is that the Vatican II reform was a reform made from above—a fairly unusual phenomenon—which was not prepared from below. Regional synods followed rather than

[9] See, for example, the encyclical *Ad Petri cathedram* of 29 June 1959 (AAS, 51—1959—511), a text which recurs in the Motu proprio *Superno Dei nutu* of 5 June 1960. And a Pentecost address of the same date in the basilica of St Peter. On 13 November 1960, on the feast of St John Chrysostom, during a mass which he was celebrating, John XXIII said: "The Council should provide the Church of Christ ... with the simple and pure lines of its origins." On the next day, when inaugurating the work of the preparatory commissions, he said: "We really expect great things of this Council. It will bring about a renewal of the forces of the Faith, of education, of ecclesiastical discipline, of religious and spiritual life, at the same time it will contribute to a reaffirmation of the principles of Christian order. ..."

preceded the Council, whereas Vatican I, far less innovatory, was preceded by several local councils, which were for their own part scarcely innovatory at all. History shows that a reform requires the commitment of all the forces of the Church. This is one of the main reasons why, historically, reforms and councils have so often been linked with one another.

The Situation Today

The crisis is of such a nature and the questions posed are so radical and so universal that one is permitted to ask whether an *aggiornamento* is enough and whether something more is not required. The question arises to the extent that the institutions of the Church are part of a cultural world which will no longer enjoy the same place in the new cultural world born of the hegemony of technology, mass media, the human sciences, and characterized by a universal secularization. We are faced by questions that are much more radical than those of the past—both from without and from within. The questions which the other Christian communions set us already put many institutions in question, but all that is now a thing of the past. The other Christian communions—those of the West at least—are now in question just as we are. We now have to take into account the criticisms voiced by priests who have left the Catholic ministry but remain attached to Christianity—Charles Davis, for example.

Others, without having renounced their Catholic priesthood, construct a radical critique of the institutions of the Church as handed down in the course of history. The standpoints of such priests are certainly open to some criticism but they pose many real questions, for example in regard to the form and style of authority in the Church. Unfortunately, political criteria are often mixed up with evangelical criteria, and the actualities of the Church are not always approached with a sufficiently inward and spiritual orientation. Young people, who are allowed to say far too little in the Church, are almost wholly allergic to anything that smacks of the institution. As soon as anything threatens to become set and a directive, it is "repressive", "alienating". Everything subsumed under the institution (which is criticized without distinguishing between the wholly relative and the inalienable) is seen as being "hypocritical", and incapable of expressing a free, spontaneous and sincere movement; the institution is also viewed as a self-justification of a Church preoccupied solely with itself, and therefore without interest for men. Here again, motivations are dominated by a political preoccupation in the widest sense of the word. The young are for a Jesus Christ who is a "man for other men". The only "Church" they will have is the collectivity of those who live the Gospel as a message of liberation and human brotherhood.

Theologically, a reformist programme derives from the ideal imposed on the Church, either in regard to its origins, or in regard to what it is called to become throughout history in the direction of eschatology. In both cases, in fact, one can and ought to criticize its present historical *forms* in order to make them conform more (and therefore reform them) to what is required by a more demanding form of faithfulness.

In the first case, those who must speak are primarily the exegetes, historians and sociologists of knowledge. Their disciplines are powerful instruments of purification and renewal, always provided one's will and spirit are open enough to a *metanoia* to allow of any reaching of conclusions. The second case —the progress in time towards eschatology—concerns the vast realm of pastoral, missionary, liturgical and scientifico-apostolic adaptation to the requirements of the age. Our epoch of rapid change and cultural transformation (philosophical ferments and sociological conditions different from those which the Church has accustomed itself to until now) calls for a revision of "traditional" forms which goes beyond the level of adaptation or *aggiornamento*, and which would be instead a new creation.[10] It is no longer sufficient to maintain, by adapting it, what has already been; it is necessary to reconstruct it.[11]

This kind of reconstruction cannot occur effectively except on

[10] "One might well ask if the time of reform is not nearing its end and if . . . the time of re-creation is not about to begin", René Pascal, *Esprit* (January 1968), p. 112.

[11] In his article "Le passion de l'Eglise", *Etudes* (October 1970), pp. 417–430, M. Légaut writes: "There is no doubt that this reorganization will be a veritable process of reconstruction, since it will not occur before the ruins have appeared. . . ." See also the same author's *Introduction à l'Intelligence du passé et de l'avenir du christianisme* (Paris, 1970).

the basis of a very determined revision of the historical character of institutions, forms and structures, and of a very genuine spiritual potential. It is a question of *transmitting*, in new forms, the same faith, the same Eucharist and the same prayer, the same ministry that the Church received and by which it has been constituted from the start. Christianity, in fact, is an "instituted" religion, in the sense in which Wach uses this expression in opposition to "natural" religion. It is essentially transmission— "tradition". One can recreate only the forms of what one has already received. In order to make the *paradosis*—the transmission—effective and authentic, this or that form in which the transmission occurred in the past, but which would nowadays be an obstacle to its reality, must eventually be revised and renewed. This is why every reform requires not only an analysis of the situation and its demands, but basic resources of a very pure kind in the form of a knowledge of the indefeasible content of the Christian realities which are to be handed on.

It often happens nowadays that sociological or psychological inquiries or a socio-political analysis take pride of place, or that two treatments are conducted on different levels without contact with one another. One example of this in regard to the celibacy of the priesthood is a treatment that develops only mystical considerations, whether they be profound or not, and a treatment offering the results of an inquiry or a psycho-sociological analysis, potentially of real value. On the one side, there is a total historicity, and on the other an a-historical position which inhibits perhaps legitimate or even necessary reforms in the name of unduly sacralized models, or of a legalism which absolutizes the rules acquired in the past. Catholics are led, even in social and political matters, to believe that there are ideal, given models, whereas social forms are to be created in variable contexts.

We must have neither a pure spirituality nor a pure sociological analysis. What is required is a union of the spirit and an effort to renew the structures.

The spirit can never wholly free itself from the structures. Today the spirit would create its own spontaneous structures—informal in the sense of not being predetermined by authority, by the directives of the group-Church, by some "total pastoral". I believe that the phenomenon of "basic groups", now considerable, is a vehicle of great positive values.[12] It is at this level, to a great extent, that the tissues of a living Christianity will be re-formed. It is here, probably, that new forms will be found for the transmission of Christian reality. But the last word is not a specific anti-institutionalism nor the ideal of a Christianity diluted like mere yeast into the dough of the age. I could not subscribe without reservations to an assertion of the following kind: "The ideal would be a Church without any specific loca-tion. . . ."[13] Declarations of this kind are made by men who enjoy all the benefits of a solidly based Church that has allowed them their education in faith and prayer. What would things be like for the second generation that took such a proposition as its starting-point? What would become of evangelization if there were no institution to bear it, feed it, and promote it? A reform should ensure that institutions serve the evangelical and mes-sianic work of Jesus; it should not dissolve them into mist. The spirit, in its biblical sense, is not opposed to the "body", but to the "earthly" and "immobile". Jesus compares it to the wind, which one cannot see even though it is shifting something (Jn. 3. 8).

[12] See my paper given at the Strasbourg colloquium on this theme in May 1971: proceedings published by CERDIC (Strasbourg, 1971).
[13] B. Besret, *Clefs pour une Eglise nouvelle* (Paris, 1971), p. 214.

Translated by John Griffiths

Karl-Heinz Ohlig

The Theological Objectives of Church Reform

THE reform of the Church is a much discussed topic. But it is often looked at one-sidedly, from the angle of the adaptation of the Church's structures, preaching, language and teaching to modern forms of society. The catchword *"aggiornamento"* (Pope John XXIII) led to demands for the reform of an antiquated ecclesiastical structure that had in many cases remained unchanged for centuries. But the opponents of reform could easily dismiss these demands as attempts at Modernism, or mere "with-it" talk, or simply a spineless craving for adaptation.

It would, however, be a simplification of the idea of church reform to imagine that it was only a matter of finding ways of bridging over the vast distance between the societies of Church and State, or of pretending that it was other than it is. Reform means, above all, the theological and spiritual renewal of the Church. Men's dissatisfaction with the Church, which leads them to demand its reform, has chiefly theological grounds: the discrepancy between what the Church, beginning in Jesus of Nazareth, was meant to be, and what it has in the course of centuries become. Christians are distressed about the Church and clamour for reform not only because they are led astray by the spirit of the times, but precisely because they are Christians, and therefore caught up in wonderment at Jesus and all that belongs to him. But when they look at the Church, they are often unable to recognize his will in it.

This discrepancy between what the Church (or, as it used to be called, the *ecclesia spiritualis*) ought to be, and what the Church (the *ecclesia visibilis*) is in actual fact, is nothing new. In principle it is unavoidable. The realization that the Gospel does not and never will fit easily into human society is part of the Gospel itself, which has been handed down by sinful men from earliest Christian times. The demand for absolute purity of teaching (orthodoxy) or of practice (orthopraxy) betrays a fanatical purism from whichever side it comes ("conservative" or "progressive"), and leads it in its turn to inhuman and un-Christian behaviour. Such a demand will stir men to fresh efforts on behalf of the Gospel only if it is accompanied by an awareness of the essential feebleness of all efforts, and of the Church as a mixture of sanctity and sinfulness. But the development within a Church can be so far-reaching that demands for reform can no longer be side-stepped or passed off by a reference to "the Church of sinners". Many in the Catholic Church feel that this point has now been reached. Overcoming Monophysite tendencies in relation to the Church is the most important prerequisite for reform today, and unfortunately its central objective. Just as Christological Monophysitism originated in a great longing to deify humanity, and thus came to misunderstand the fundamental nature of poverty and the cross in relation to Jesus and Christians, and the enduring element of hope in the Christian faith, so a related ecclesiological Monophysitism similarly denies, on seemingly religious grounds, the sinful side of the Church. It refuses to see faith in God and salvation in Jesus Christ as a hope that is not yet realized, visible and proved.

Such thinking identifies at one and the same level the concrete Church with the mystical Body of Christ. Thus all central claims made by the Church turn triumphally into divine rights. And the dogma of the Church in its historical aspect becomes eternal truth. The traditions of the Church are considered sacrosanct. The concrete forms of ecclesiastical office, and the entire ecclesiastical structure that has developed over the centuries, are held to be divinely instituted. The teaching office turns into an "infallible" channel of the Holy Spirit. Church law is to a large extent and without careful examination equated with divine law (*ius divinum*). In the sacraments, God himself is thought to function, directly. In short, God, his will, his Spirit, are identified with the Church and its practices in a way that makes reform impossible, or at any rate makes it very much more difficult. In this view, even serious questioning, for example, Hans Küng's on infallibility), or discussion (for example, on celibacy), are made to seem irreverent and rebellious. Christian people and priests who show eagerness for reform are treated like impious and ultimately even unbelieving members of the Church—because they cast doubt on the guidance of the Spirit.

The concepts mentioned above (guidance of the Spirit, infallibility, *ius divinum*, etc.) are not simply to be discarded at this point as harmful. But their light-hearted and casual use in discussion must be shown up as a form of latent Monophysitism seeking to do away with the fundamental and permanent distinction between the (hoped-for) divine and the (given) human. Just as, according to the teaching of the Council of Chalcedon, the divinity and humanity of Christ are inseparable, yet each remains itself unmixed with the other, and faith in the divinity of Jesus (whatever is understood thereby) does not make this divinity a natural and historical component of his humanity, so the statements about the guidance of the Spirit or the infallibility of the Church cannot turn these, in their *historical* reality, into quasi-natural emanations of the divine will. Such thinking would only have the appearance of religions—in reality it would tend towards the idolatry of human history, and would nullify all true hope of salvation (including that of the Church). Hence the dogma of Chalcedon must be integrated into the ecclesiology and practice of the Church. Only in this way will the path be open for free critical thought and discussion, from which no aspect of the Church need be excluded.

The faith and practice of the Church are derived from tradition. We must never forget this. Reform that seeks simply to break with the past, ignoring history, and wants to make a totally fresh start, without any attempt at continuity, would be denying its own necessities and could not therefore be a reform of the *Church*. Just as tradition and the present-day Church which grew from it are neither of them sacrosanct, so the reform movement cannot start from a definitive judgment of the Church's past. In fact we must refrain from self-righteous judgments and recognize that the Christians of the past always tried to fashion the Church anew, that they too wanted to create, however fragmentarily like ourselves, the true Church of Christ. We must accept that they, too, were in possession of true faith and hope and the love that comes from the Spirit of God—at least whenever the Church spoke as one in faith and act. It may be that the teaching of the "infallibility" of statements agreed on by the whole Church concerning faith and morals can be understood as precisely this fundamental and uncritical oneness of present-day Christians with the Church of the past.

But this very solidarity with the "faith of our fathers", and the acceptance of tradition as a challenge to our understanding, does not by any means imply that we must simply repeat or imitate the behaviour of past Christians. Tradition will not be satisfied by idolatry or by a sterile imitation of the past, but only by the courageous shaping of a future that grows out of it. Only thus will tradition be handed on in any real sense to new generations.

The "faith of the fathers" on which the Church bases itself is not—and this must not be forgotten—the faith of conformers and traditionalists, but of people who were in conflict with the religious and social systems of their time, who abandoned them in the name of God, and went forward to new frontiers. From Abraham on, who left the land of his fathers and his gods at the word of God, believing in a far-off promise, the "exodus", the departure from the old and traditional, and the "desert", the total poverty and indefinable hidden experience of God, have become the type of Israel's religious life. The God without image, whom they were not even allowed to call by name, continually forced them to break away from the familiar traditions in which they felt at home. In the name of this *true* tradition of faith in Yahweh, the prophets attempted over and over again to make present this Yahweh in worship, law and institution. In *this* tradition stands Jesus of Nazareth with his condemnation of received late-Jewish practice, and his preaching of the God who is so totally different from the image that has been handed down of him. The key to his preaching, following close on prophetic tradition, is the conversion of man, his re-thinking, and that means a departure from traditional forms of life and thought, and a readiness to enter upon the new.

The Christian faith, therefore, rests on a tradition of the non-traditional. We should not be remaining true to the spirit of the fathers if we limited it to examples that had to be imitated, and turned its teaching into a rigid system to which we had to conform. Throughout history we find the true tradition among men and women who freed their Church from the strait-jacket of the past and led it on to new paths—people like Paul, Augustine, Francis of Assisi, Thomas Aquinas, Luther, and so on, right up to John XXIII. It is precisely this appeal to Church tradition that leads to critical re-thinking and courageous reform. Criticism and reform are part of the essence of the Church of Jesus Christ. His Spirit is not confined by law and the letter of the law—it is a spirit that makes free.

The New Testament sayings about the unworthy servants (Luke 17. 10), about the salt of the earth that loses its taste and is no longer good for anything except to be trodden underfoot by men (Mt. 5. 13), and about the necessity of taking up one's cross and following Christ (Mark 8. 34), right up to the inevitability of death if the grain of wheat is to bear fruit (John 12. 24) and the hatred of one's own life (John 12. 25), have in the past been chiefly applied personally to individual Christians. But these sayings must *also*, and perhaps primarily, be understood as directed to the community of disciples, the Church. Following Christ demands from the Church the constant readiness to give up everything that has become dear to it over the course of time—its traditions, all that it holds to be its life, and to walk in poverty beneath the cross towards the hope of new life.

In order to reform the Church, it is not enough to re-think one's theology in this sense: that is, to bring about a changed awareness. Criticism and reform must find a place for themselves within the structure of the Church. Institutions must be created which will make continued development possible. This is necessary not only—by contrast with earlier times—because of the speed-up of changes within society (including that of the Church), but above all by reason of the increased socialization of human life and the enormous possibilities of manipulation on the part of established authority. In the face of this unforeseen increase in power (which also includes the power of the Church), the critical and reforming methods used up to now (for example, the selfless involvement of exceptional individuals from the Orders and theological schools) will be useless. In view of this, the demand for the institutionalization of criticism and reform seems (also) to be a *theological* necessity.

Further development will make clear what such an institution may come to look like. In any case the chief things to be taken into consideration here are as follows: (1) It must be recognized that public opinion and the instruments it employs (a critical and free press, etc.) have their own special function in the Church; (2) measures must be taken to control power at all levels in the Church; (3) there must be a firm demarcation of authority institutionally set up (for example, the exercise of hierarchical office should be made dependent on the vote of Synods; and that of ecclesiastical justice independent of the hierarchy, and so on). Further points are: The election of officials "from below"; limitations on the duration of office; development of Church law so that the individual Christian can obtain the protection of the law itself (and is not exclusively dependent on mercy), and so on.

These considerations are really no more than basic presuppositions for a possible reform of the Church. But such a reversal of habits formed in the past and nurtured by the authorities of the Church leads to reappraisals which, together with their institutional consequences, form the central goal and most important stage of any reform. Only thus can a process of collective, truth-seeking ideas be given theological and practical content and lead to the attempt to find ways to realization.

Within the Catholic Church there are a multitude of theological and moral systems, and many kinds of understanding of what church membership implies. There is no such thing as *one* Catholic theology or *one* Catholic theologian. Thus the theological objectives resulting from this pluralism are extremely various, colourful and often contradictory. This applies even to such small communities as the parish, the diocese, or the province. How much more then to the far larger sphere of the universal Church, where the most diverse social and cultural groups, and ages, co-exist with one another?

To introduce reform into the Church only when there has been reached—over this entire vast area—at least some measure of agreement would be tantamount to giving up most kinds of reform altogether. It is possible to imagine a certain sacral and ritualistic understanding of Christianity, the Church, ecclesiastical office or the sacraments, among the inhabitants of Southern Italy or Africa, which has become meaningless to the people of Northern Europe or North America. In the former instance premature reforms could possibly do violence to the Christian conscience; but in the latter, new institutions might already be long overdue. To reserve certain peripheral theological questions concerning reform (e.g., the structures of the Church, or celibacy) to the central authority would also be theologically incorrect, because obligatory reform would either not be introduced at all, or —in the case of certain areas—introduced too early, or of the majority, too late. Allowing decisions to be made at a lower level, and referring them to higher authority only when this is impossible, seems to be a theological necessity.

For the same reason, an exhaustive treatment, or even only a full list of the concrete theological objectives of a possible reform in the Church, cannot be made by one person alone. The plurality of aims arising out of the various ecclesiastical specifications is too great. Hence it is not my intention to attempt a necessarily very one-sided catalogue of such objectives. I mean only to consider the principal aims and guide-lines of any conceivable reform. Starting from what the Church essentially is, from its beginnings, and allowing for all subjective limitations, I will endeavour to show, in theological terms, the great dynamic trend in men's efforts on its behalf.

The Church is the Church of Christ. It grew out of his preaching and his life. It sees itself as the group of his disciples who have followed him and all he stands for wholeheartedly; for whom he is their final hope, the culmination of man's "history with God", and who, in following Christ, will be realizing this hope. This divine hope brought by Jesus is what the Church preaches in history, until the Lord comes again.

The Church therefore is essentially the group of Jesus' followers. Jesus the Lord (or God in Jesus) is thus the only principle of life and validity that the Church possesses. And every reform must strive to make the preaching of Jesus as Lord more effective and more credible. This must be its only theological goal. The reform of the Church must turn it more and more into the Church of Jesus Christ. The reform of the Church has from the very beginning a Christological objective.

The principal criticism of the Church on the part of committed Christians starts from the fact that it puts too much weight on itself, its understanding of itself, its structures and its traditions. Much of what it says concerns the definition of its own rights, the defence of ecclesiastical structures and practices, the preservation of the *status quo*. For example, almost all Roman promulgations, announcements and projects of the last few years, excepting only the appeals for peace and utterances on social questions, come under this heading. The ordinary Christian simply cannot any longer understand what all these things have to do with the message of Christ, and how his hope, grounded in Jesus, can be fulfilled by them. The Church seems like a powerful, self-mirroring and self-sufficient machine that is no longer capable of orientating itself on Jesus and letting itself be questioned by him.

The belief of Christians, that the authority of the Lord stands behind the Church and all it does, is not always correctly understood. The Church speaks with authority from the Lord only if and to the extent that it preaches the Lord. Not every utterance of the Church has the support of Christ's authority, for if it had, then all further discussion would be meaningless. The Church has authority only in so far as it claims no power for itself but refers everything it does to the authority of Jesus. The Church's rights are solely those of selfless service in the preaching of Jesus Christ. It has to be poor in the sense that it can claim nothing for itself.

Every claim, therefore, that the Church makes must be founded in Jesus, or it has no validity at all. The Church can make binding pronouncements only in the ultimate sense of confessing Christ, as Peter did, and submitting itself to him. But if the Church thinks in "human" terms, and puts the preservation of its own existence before everything else, then it becomes an enemy. This dialectical tension (as expressed in Mt. 16. 18 and 16. 23) cannot be resolved.

Referring everything the Church is to Christ is not only consoling but obligatory—a task to be undertaken ever anew.

Theology's purpose is to explain how everything in the Church has to be centred on Christ. The unity of the Church (churches) is present where Christ (and nothing else) is preached. If the churches preach themselves, their understanding of themselves, their structures, then divisions will occur. Christian churches should—in the strictly theological sense—have no awareness of themselves at all, but only of Jesus. Unity is present where the churches do not rely on their own traditions and ideas, but only on Jesus. The sacraments are not simply the self-fulfilment of the Church but, more basically, the confession by the individual in the Christian community of Jesus as Lord, and of the hope promised in him. (Thus baptism, for example, is not primarily the reception of the individual into the Christian Church but, more fundamentally, the confession of Jesus and of the hope of an eschatological solidarity in salvation with all men through God. The individual who dares aspire to this hope, in Jesus' name, by becoming a member of the Christian community through baptism, is of secondary importance. And it is the same with the other sacraments.)

Ecclesiastical office must not be grounded exclusively in a hierarchical structure "willed by God", but, more fundamentally, in the service of others, in order to open up to them the possibilities of faith and love that Jesus has made available. The "extraordinary" teaching office, Church law, divine worship, and so on—all these must be understood more radically, in the sense of their usefulness in the service of preaching Jesus, the Christ.

Reform in practice must aim to bring about a concrete realization of the presence of Jesus in everything the Church is and does; and to make credible what theology has to say about him as the one and only Lord. Collective attempts must be made to find new ways of bringing about the realization of the exclusively Jesus-centred character of office, sacrament, worship, law—in short, of the Church as socio-political reality.

Above all, however, we have to consider that the Lord preached by the Church is not simply an object of cult or abstract speculation but the *historical* Jesus of Nazareth. Faith in the risen Lord is not possible if one does not adhere to Jesus. To confess Jesus as Lord means to take his "concerns", the things he lived for and died for, with utter seriousness and to try to practise them. The "conservative" polemic directed against talk of "the thing of Jesus" fails to see that this polemic can easily become an excuse to turn aside from Jesus altogether, and to make one's final authority no longer Jesus himself, but a dogmatic formulation about him. (Thus he himself becomes an extremely unimportant element in his own story.) For example, one learns a great deal in dogmatic manuals about ideas of Jesus that have been produced in the course of centuries, and very little about Jesus himself and his will. Yet God's revelation came to pass in Jesus, the word of God, and not in some dogmatic formulation or other. Formulations are no more than human responses to Jesus, the attempts of Christian generations to express their relationship to him. The dogma of the Church does not exist for its own sake, but only to point in a straight line to Jesus. It is man's confession of him, put into words. Dogma, however, is not primarily realized in the repetition of a form of words, but in the acceptance of Jesus as Lord.

It is the historical Jesus and none other who is the Lord of the Church, the centre of everything that exists in the Church. To live in the spirit of God means to live in the spirit of Jesus. The guidance of the Holy Spirit in the Church is not, therefore, an automatic, supernatural guarantee of all the Church does. The Spirit of the Lord has historical implications. It is given wherever the things of Jesus are put first—in the midst of all doubts and pluralities of meaning that are inseparable from life in history. Jesus and the things of Jesus are the historical criteria to which the Church must cling if it does not want to fall away from the Spirit. (Jesus' promise allows the Church to hope that a total break in continuity with its Lord will not occur.) Reliance on the Holy Spirit is identical with hopeful adherence to the things of Jesus.

These considerations lead to two practical consequences for Church practice and reform—the importance of relying on the authority and critical function of Holy Scripture as the norm for all ecclesiastical utterances in theory and practice. Because—purely historically—there is no other approach to Jesus save by the Bible (the Old Testament as the pre-history of Jesus, without which he cannot be understood in his historical outline; and the New Testament as the collection of Jesus traditions, and the thoughts that came from the communities that were closest to him historically), the Bible is the criterion for all the Church does. Dogma, law, and the pastoral objectives set before us are binding in so far as they derive from Scripture and—in a new spiritual and historical, and political, situation—give fresh insights into it.

Using this criterion is not simple. The individual Christian has no "Catholic principle of Scripture" by which to judge as ultimately binding, from some Archimedean point outside the Church, the Church's own pronouncements. On the other hand, the official assertion that these are supported by Scripture cannot stop him making his own critical judgments. Hence everything done or said by the Church must be subjected to continuous public discussion in order to show clearly that it accords with Scripture or is related in its Christian relevance to some aspect emerging from Scripture. It necessarily follows, moreover, from the confession of the historical Jesus as Lord, that the things for which he lived and died must somehow be realized in the Church, however fragmentarily. The life of Jesus may be difficult to examine historically, hidden as it is in the dark recesses of history, but his central aims are very well understood, not least through recent researches into his life. These are: his preaching of the Kingdom of God, that is, his firm hope in a successful outcome of human history through the mercy of God; in humanity, mercy, peace and human happiness. And following from this the fundamental importance and divine value of man, the absolute rejection of all that threatens to ruin man and human life, the readiness to risk his own life for his message; and the hope, expressed in his acceptance of death on the cross, that life, his own and all human life, has a meaning transcending history, and so on. The Church, its doctrines, its structures, its worship, office and law must be renewed in such a way that Christ's preaching becomes meaningful to the world of today. The Church must strive to show in all it does that it, like Jesus, cares about man; that it wants to give concrete service to his hopes; that it, more than other social groups, will stubbornly oppose those who deprive him of his rights, who threaten and oppress and torment him.

But such witness to the Spirit of Christ cannot be made credible while freedom, human rights and human dignity are only talked about when they are being endangered *outside* the Church. For the Church, too, has in the course of centuries permitted and perpetrated within its own domain many sorts of inhumanity, and created divisions and disputes within itself. People have been and are oppressed by it in various ways, humiliated and disappointed in their hopes. Its call to the world must not remain on the verbal level, but must consist above all in the imitation and realization of the things of Jesus.

The overcoming of an ecclesiastical Monophysitism, and with it the readiness to accept the sinful aspects of the Church and to take up the cross, the referring back to Jesus of all the Church is and does, with all the consequences that this entails—these seem to be the basic objectives of church reform, considered theologically. Only within this framework can all other concrete objectives (the oneness of the Church, the abandonment of all sterile, dogmatic thinking, the humanizing of church law, the importance placed on the "political" responsibility of the Church, etc.) find their validity, and show that they naturally follow from an ever newly reiterated and solely justifying confession of Christ. It is only at this point that it becomes clear that an *aggiornamento* of the Church is more than simply a practical necessity. It is also a *theological* requirement. For Jesus cannot be confessed as 'Lord", and become the catalyst of concrete hopes, except through contemporary modes of speech and thought.

Reducing everything in the Church to Christ is especially urgent today because "God", "religion" and "tradition" are no longer automatically understood. In times of far-reaching (and continuing) secularization of personal and social life, the churches could have their accepted place simply as "religious communities", so that theory and practice could be active in many peripheral spheres. The Church could develop a rich interior life. Men strong enough to occupy themselves with secondary things could make these central and dispute them.

Today, many Christians of all confessions are confronted in their daily life by the simple yet, for Christians, fundamental question: Can they in fact believe in Jesus of Nazareth, and in the hope brought by him? In face of this question, many other things that have for long been considered important fade into the background. To give brotherly service to doubting men is the duty of the churches, the community of those who confess Jesus as the Christ, despite all temptations, and with courage. To develop structures that will make such service possible and effective must be the task of the reformers of the Church.

Translated by Erika Young

Alois Müller

Practical Theology of Church Reform

REFORM of the Church is a theological problem because the Church can be proficiently understood by no means other than the theological: that is, by cognition proceeding from faith.

But the Church is a social body corporate; hence its reform is a sociological problem as well.

Other problems are involved in the question of church reform, such as the dialectic of spirit and structure, of multiplicity and unity, or of concord and conflict. All these aspects have to be considered if a "practical theology of church reform" is to be developed: the answer, that is, to the question: How is the now requisite reform of the Church to be implemented?

This "plan for a practical theology of church reform" already implies a question: To what extent is reform something that *can be* planned and consciously carried through? The answer will in its turn lead to the question of the vehicles and the process of church reform. These are the basic lines of approach if one is to apprehend the contents and the practice of a reform of the Church at the present time.

I. Is Church Reform practicable?

There is a certain mistrust of a planned church reform. It is held to be a piece of human presumption, an attempt of *homo faber* to tackle a field outside his competence. A reform of the Church is expected to come from the action of grace and of the Spirit, and prayer is said to be the sole appropriate effort that can be made to that end.

This sort of opinion considers one specific aspect of church reform—the question of the "renewal of spirit", and even sees that
only in relation to its transcendent ground. We should not forget
this aspect, for there is a transcendent foundation for a renewal
of the spirit of members of the Church; yet it is not the whole
reality. The transcendent ground takes effect in immanent causes,
and the spirit needs structure: the structure of thought and the
(social) structure of effect. But that brings us into the realm of
the plannable and practicable.

This means, too, that when we speak of plannable and practicable church reform, it is essentially a question of structural
reform. Then the renewal of spirit as the *conditio sine qua non*,
indeed as the basic cause of the whole phenomenon, is neither
overlooked nor put to one side; instead the question of reform is
tackled on a level where it is a matter of the humanly plannable
and practicable.

But it would be equally wrong to conceive church reform
solely on the model of practicability. It cannot be constructed in
model form in an office, for it is an interhuman process occurring
in behaviour patterns and social structures: a process of permanent
interhuman and spiritua, psychological and social confrontation
and interaction.

Of course, a will to reform does imply planning structures
and working out models, but means just as much the instigation
of thought processes, stimulation of psychological processes, and
release of social developments, for which there is none of that
"timing" so dear to the managerial mind.

An appropriate thought at the commencement of a practical
theology of church reform is that it is not "totally plannable",
but has a dimension which is open to planning, which we neglect
only at our peril. Instead of, or in addition to, the "planning"
model, that of "education" should be adduced: it is a matter of
spiritual and mental processes of influence and development in
a psychological, sociological and "political" mode of time, but
not a mathematico-mechanical time. Structural measures, the introduction or abrogation of laws—arrangements—have their
place in this process, but they cannot be applied just like that,
without recourse to the whole process of reform.

II. The Vehicles and Process of Church Reform

A. *Who makes the Reforms?*

If the "dialectic of spirit and structure", church reform as a "non-totally plannable phenomenon with a plannable dimension", is invoked, then on the one hand we hear all about the magisterium and its prerogatives, and on the other hand about "free charisms", the "people of God", the *ecclesia* and its competence. Here we run the danger of an ideological, theologically coloured *a priori*: either one is determined from the start to accord everything to the hierarchy and nothing to the church community, and one deduces everything desirable from the teaching of the magisterium until the actual conclusions correspond to the *a priori*; or one decides to diminish the power of the office and derive an appropriate theological instrument from the people-of-God ecclesiology. In both cases, the error consists of attempting a theological knock-out in a case which is certainly environed by theological realities but which has primarily non-theological dimensions.

1. Since everything that can come under a reform of the Church has an empirical dimension, shared by all participants, all participants *can* see whether this or that phenomenon of church life is functioning appropriately or requires reform. Of course the criteria for this judgment are *partly* theological in nature, but since theology is a thought process, its arguments are also fundamentally applicable and verifiable.

It is a question of sheer fact whether a member, or a group of members, of the Church has the requisite knowledge of appropriate functioning or of need for reform in any particular question of church practice (including the practice of proclamation, or that of theological reflection). Since education (even theological formation) and expertise generally develop slowly (though steadily), in the Church today we also have to take into account a more widespread adjustment of the way in which problems and requisite reforms are understood. The church community (its individual members who are without any specific office; that is, the basis) is to be credited nowadays with considerable "expert" knowledge.

The objection that this would imply neglect of the supernatural dimension, that judgment in ecclesiastical and theological matters is an affair not only of logical thought but of supernatural illumination, of leadership by the Holy Spirit, is fallacious. One side will use theological arguments to reserve this "office" essentially to the leadership, whereas the other will seek to show theologically that the Holy Spirit also takes effect in the entire people of God, and so on. But here some correction is necessary. It is a theologumenon (and certainly a transcendent reality) that the Spirit operates in the official and non-official members of the Church. But even this transcendent action is translated into the empirical dimension of the understandable and visible: that is, of cognitive cut-and-thrust. Of course, this applies only within a horizon of understanding which is marked out by faith and itself stamped by the spirit of the Gospel. Within this horizon, however, the decisive dispute takes place about what is ecclesiastically just and proper.

But, even here, exactly where in the Church the most appropriate ideas on reform are to be conceived, is a question of fact.

2. Judicial competence is distinguished from that of expertise. In decision we have the specifically institutional component. If expertise is essentially something diffuse, judicial competence produces the uniformity of the social structure: whoever belongs to it knows what is right and proper within this whole; to submit to judicial competence produces membership and allegiance; a reciprocal identification results.

Expertise and judicial competence cannot, however, be wholly divorced one from the other. That the judiciary need expertise is obvious. But it is also true that, by the very nature of the whole process, expertise tends to share in judicial competence. This is probably a major cause of the present "fundamental democratization": in the long run, it is not humanly tenable that expertise should not participate in decisions which can in their turn affect that expertise.

The theological objection here is that judicial competence in the Church is by "divine right" vouchsafed to the hierarchy, and that no expertise, however proficient, can endow a member or part of the Church not holding office with the right to judicial competence. But this, too, is a wrong appreciation of the theological actuality. The fact that the formal locus of competence for a decision in the Church is always the one who also most "in-tensively" represents the Church formally and institutionally, i.e., the office-holder or holders, does not mean that no one else can participate in the process of arriving at the decision that the office-holder enunciates; it does not mean that the office-holder must discover the decision by himself, or that in every case he alone possesses the moral right to deny all others any influence on that decision.

In short: the Catholic teaching on the ecclesiastical magis-terium, according to which only that asserted by the magisterium has an "official" character, in no way prejudices the inclusion of non-official members of the Church in the process of reflection and decision. The impulse to church reform can therefore arise fundamentally from the non-official community, and the ques-tion of alliance with the Spirit is decided not at this initial point but rather in the fruits of the process.

3. But there is also the question whether a development or a reform is permissible only if it ultimately wins the approval of the magisterium. Or could (should) there also be developments in the Church which ultimately produce universally effective results, but without official approval, despite the magisterium? The reference to implicit approval, when there is no express con-tradiction or objection from the magisterium, does not wholly resolve the problem. There would seem to be developments which to a certain extent occur under protest or deprecation from the hierarchy, and yet bring about such results. Here we ought to consider to what extent such a social body really exists only by virtue of the official norms. Of course a social entity cannot pro-ceed without official norms. But not all its existential processes depend on such standards. There is a form of non-officially con-trolled dependence on a behavioural equilibrium which is ulti-mately an inalienable part of social reality. In so far as this may help further to develop the official norms, it may ultimately be characterized as an authentic expression of the existing social entity.

In theological terms, this means (as far as the Church is con-cerned): even in spontaneous processes occurring in the people of God, the Spirit of Christ can be at work (charisms), and even developments which are not comprehended in an official process of enunciation can be authentic church reform. The office and official activity are not the adequate sum of all that which occurs in the Church in social reality and at the behest of the Spirit.

In this regard there is in a social entity a healthy functional equilibrium that can be "pathologically" disturbed, either by way of an increasing tension and discrepancy between official and unofficial norms, or by way of a deficit of spontaneous processes, and a reduction of life to the official system of norms. In the Church, the alternative should not be sought between these two pathological states, but in the condition of healthy homeostasis.

B. *How are Reforms brought about?*

I have already referred to the fact that church reform is not simply plannable and practicable. Yet it must be stated that the greater complexity now existing, together with the simultaneous greater elucidation of social processes that is possible, makes an optimally conscious and controlled action indispensable. No one today can develop the Church "on his own". All those responsible must co-operate in the process of planning the necessary reforms. Accordingly, both the official and non-official members of the Church are involved in the process in terms of their specific contributions.

1. A planned church reform means first of all a *strategy for reform*, and therefore a concept of the main lines and areas of the development envisaged. This strategy has to take into account the variation of stages and of emphases in requisite reforms in the different part-churches. It tries to establish a picture of the whole in space and in time, and from this to draw the far-reaching conclusions which may mean that the individual has, when necessary, to wait in the interests of the whole. The reform strategy also includes plans which are perhaps impracticable at the moment, but whose time will come.

2. Not every plan for reform can be carried out in this way. There is a variety among reform methods which must always be taken into consideration. Here the following questions are important: Central or decentralized control? Control by means of binding decrees or by suggestion and incitement? Conclusive regulation or free development—possibly with an experimental

stage in the narrower sense? It should be remarked that the method of the Roman reforms shows a certain oscillation between more restrictive forms (central, binding regulations) and more open variations (local responsibilities, mere guide-lines, and so on).

3. Finally, a reform must declare itself in terms of actual reformist *measures*. These are what every member of the Church directly apprehends as what is different, as what the reform is. Conditioned by the reform objective, built into the reform strategy, put into practice with a method appropriate to the reform, the individual measure is therefore the "ultimate" reform. Paradoxically, it is also to some extent the most relative aspect of reform.

The reciprocal dependence of the measure and the goal of reform can be a mere possibility: the mere introduction and practice of a specific reformist measure do not guarantee that the desired goal has been reached. The reform could go wrong, and be short-sightedly confused with the external measures taken.

III. Working Hypotheses on Church Reform Today

"The reform of the Second Vatican Council has slipped out of the hands of the church leadership." This perhaps excessive proposition is not intended to shock but as a neutral observation of the fact that one phase in which reform appeared to be the work and decree of the magisterium has been followed by a phase in which it relies on spontaneous tendencies originating in the church community and "by-passing" the magisterium.

There are certain reasons why this has happened, but it is now rather wearisome to list them yet again. It is more important to try to interpret the future consequences of this fact (once the theological limitations have been defined). An "official" reform can lead more speedily to clear and binding results, yet it is actively hindered by many ecclesio-sociological factors. A reform arising from the community has more prospects of being creative, but it does run the risk of remaining non-binding and diffuse. Today the Church is in a kind of creatively diffuse phase of reform, with all the chances and risks that that entails. At the same time it is in an increasingly fluid stage ("dissolution", some would say) as far as institutions are concerned, in which little that is "decided" can really any longer appear. That the situation has certain unfortunate aspects is incontestable. But it is also permissible to assert that this "running temperature" is necessary if that necessary fluidity is to occur (throughout the whole structure of the Church) without which developments and reforms necessary for the future could not occur. In any case, we have to start with this situation today, if we are to reflect upon the task for reform in the future.

A. *Reform of the Understanding of Faith*

It is often said today that this or that phenomenon in the Church indicates—"essentially"—a crisis of faith. It may also be said that the whole situation of the Church today is a crisis of faith. Yet this word must be correctly understood. An inadequate diagnosis would confirm a lack of ready belief, "subjection of the understanding to the word of God". It is much more a question of a crisis of *understanding of faith*, which was inevitable.

1. The development of understanding of the Bible had to lead to the question of a hermeneutics of revelation, of the "discourse of faith". These are not things which are just up to the choice—let alone the pious humility—of those who have acknowledged the research work in question. Findings cannot be proficiently examined without offending inner truthfulness. They can no longer be simply "made to fit" the Bible, as was once tried when biblical "pre-history" was allegedly made to approximate natural and historical science. It is a matter of another kind of understanding, of what actually we receive as God's word, and hence not of decomposition and liquidation, but of the preservation of the unique quality of the word of the Bible, but in a new way. The word of God was formerly apprehended *in* the objective actuality of stories, laws and prophecies; and that objectivity was itself often confused with the word of God. Today we have been made wise to this confusion, and have to do without so easy an identification of the word.

This means that the understanding of faith changes almost like a kaleidoscope, but that individual goals (that for the sake of which Christians always believed) appears all the more clearly. Yet, in a way, everything is restructured.

This process will be basic to the future of the Church. It is evident here and there in Western civilization at the moment. But it will become universal, precisely because the scientific rationality of Western thought is the feature that will be adopted most quickly by other cultures. But it is a process that can hardly be carried through by decree. It must take root in catechetical discourse and spread from the pulpit to pastoral letters, encyclicals and conciliar documents. Of course this process would be made much easier if it were to occur not under the suspicion but with the encouragement of responsible figures in the Church.

2. This new understanding of the message of faith of the Church means that the question of the identification and comparison of faith is posed differently. Who (still) has the Catholic faith? Is this other faith compatible with the Catholic faith? And so on. These questions remain but are posed in another way. It is no longer possible to apply criteria for the verification of belief, when they have become non-objective and pointless in regard to belief itself. There are those who are convinced that there are vast numbers of "heretics" in the Catholic Church today, and that there just isn't anyone any longer with the courage to tell them what they are. This kind of thinking is conceived wholly in the terms of the past. The question of the "correctness" of an understanding of the faith has itself to be researched anew together with that of the essential nature of the understanding of faith.

This is very important in ecumenism. All churches start from certain circumscriptions of their faith which presuppose an old understanding. Differences become apparent in dialogue. But can they really be defined as "divisive in terms of faith" in contrast to those differences apparent within a church? The problem should have consequences for ecumenical dialogue, for a community of sacraments, common pastorals, and so on. In this area the most obvious tendency today is that of the above-mentioned melting-down process and attempts at reform which "by-pass" the official channels. Though it is not as if this last were in itself desirable. And it is not to be explained exclusively as a disillusioned reaction to the office-holders themselves, who "just don't want to see". It is, perhaps, just that the actual problems make any other reaction impossible on either side. It is important that there should be no break in contact between creative, innovatory groups and church officials, which would mean once again some kind of circumscription and loss of specific identity for such initiatives (what, for example, does "inter"-communion mean between those who represent nothing and no one?).

3. The new understanding of faith is bound up with a wholly new relationship between faith and the Beyond. In the old understanding faith was by and large oriented to the Beyond, and morality to the here and now.

Faith said that the Christian should strive to attain to an everlasting homeland, the only real divine goal; whereas morality said how one ought to behave in the earthly first stage of eternal life, in order to remain worthy of eternal life. Here it is not so much a question of a more ascetic turning from the world, or of a more joyful attitude to creation. Both aspects have been emphasized in the Church in all ages. What is really new today is that the promise of faith itself is understood as applying primarily to existence pure and simple, hence first of all to earthly life, so that the eternal completion, as the "absolute future of God", is carefully recorded, and indeed subscribed to, but does not stand in the foreground and does not invite us to transcend the present. Salvation for *this* life is to love one's brother together with Christ; to remain good under suffering; and so to stay truly free from all "powers" (from all "alienation"), because Christ proclaimed God to us as the absolute horizon of hope.

And, again, one image suggests another: Christian faith as a transcendent indication for this life, dependent just as much on the reality of God and the absoluteness of his turning to men, but with the focus on the here and now.

This quite new understanding of faith appears to be indispensable for any real advance and fruitfulness in the Church. When it is appreciated, and for both "friend and foe" is strong enough to banish suspicion of a mere warmed-up rationalistic liberalism, it is the fundamental reform which the Church needs at present.

B. *Reform of the Understanding of the Cult*

The first reform of the liturgy was to some extent the *belle époque* of church reform. It was the first breakthrough at the

Council, and concerned an area which was visible to all members of the Church, and despite all progressiveness remained in a theologically secure framework.

In the meantime, the field of liturgy has not remained one of idle joy. There is no real point here in getting worked up about all the obstructions to post-conciliar reform. More profound problems confront us. We are faced by these questions: Is present-day man really liturgically minded? Has the cult any legitimate place in Christianity?

1. The tendencies connected with the slogans of "desacralization", "religionless Christianity" and "secularization" have brought an important consideration under discussion: The message of Christ is the message of the "humanization" of God. God's Son wants to meet us in every man, in the least of our brothers; and what God requires of us, and what honours him, is our loving orientation to our fellow man. Instead of the circle apart in which God was honoured by cultic actions, the whole of life is for the Christian the location in which God is honoured by love for man. The Lord's Supper is no longer valuable because here and nowhere else God is "sacrificed to", but because it is (in the community of brothers) the lasting re-constitution of the Church in its unity with Christ and its mission, on the basis of his suffering and by way of the sacrament of his sacrifice on the cross. If there is so express a polarity as the following: life derived from faith as the only serious instance of Christ-dependent reference to God, and the celebration of the Eucharist as the symbolic assurance that this life is grounded in Christ, then the liturgy obtains quite another specific value than when it is uniformly, so to speak, the locus of the whole Christian relationship to God.

2. Our solemn offices, ordinary and festive celebrations—in short, all liturgies which brought together a large number of people—were structurally powered essentially by the idea of the public cultic action, which was also to a considerable extent objectified and independent of the individuals celebrating. The reform of the liturgy, however, had co-celebration by the individual as its guiding idea. This has led to the now widespread feeling of "schizophrenia": In larger eucharistic assemblies one feels that the personal elements (the kiss of peace, etc.) fall flat, whereas in smaller assemblies the rubricistic rules are always

experienced as obstacles and sources of distance. The logic of the "cultic relativization" of the Eucharist, the approximation of cult and life in the structure of the celebration of the Eucharist itself, led to a preference for the small celebration. Like that of all individual aspects, its logic is one-sided and incomplete. If other (ecclesiological but also sociological) aspects are taken into consideration, the large, "anonymous" celebration seems to me also to be proper under certain (frequently present) conditions. But cultic awareness as a whole, and its specific value in faith as a whole, have already changed considerably within the Church; reflections on the liturgy must now be directed both to the legal and to the practical aspects of this new consciousness.

C. *Reform of the Structure of the Church*

The problems of reform become most actual in the case of the structure of the Church: that is, of the Church in so far as it is a social body. These questions are objectively urgent, for alterations in human social structures have occurred whose effects on the Church must be delayed no longer; they are subjectively urgent, since, for the same reason, the awareness of social structures or social processes is acutely alive today. On the one hand, it is a question of structures and processes within the Church; and, on the other, of the relation of the Church to society.

1. When discussing the question of the vehicles of church reform, I referred to the relationship between the office and the community; now this problem is posed as an object of reform. In Catholic thinking, words play a decisive role: one acquires and then clings to them. The word "service" came into use (once again) for the hierarchy, and now seems indispensable whenever the subject is raised. Yet the actual state of discussion shows that not much is actually achieved by the word. If "service" is interpreted merely in the moral sense as gentleness and personal devotion in the fulfilment of the hierarchical office, then—however worthy the notion—it doesn't really answer the specific need. There are hierarchs who combine exceptional personal humility with wholly authoritarian direction. It is not enough to utter a word; the matter itself must be comprehended as proficiently as possible: in the magisterium—the hierarchy—absolutist and paternalistic behaviour patterns in regard to the community must

be replaced by democratic and co-operative modes. "Absolutist" means a decision and form of government without communication with those concerned. One is (or thinks one is) "informed", but there is no dialogue. Petitions are received, and rescripts are issued. This "one-way communication" prevents any actual community between hierarchy and community. "Paternalistic" is more a popular psychological expression and denotes a relationship in which the other is not treated as an adult, equal, fellow human being.

These are the behaviour patterns which as a result of the *social* maturation process are no longer acceptable in the Church. I have already shown that the theology of the magisterium is not affected by this consideration, and cannot therefore be used as an alibi. A form of government in the Church in which those affected cannot make the contribution proper to their abilities is futureless. In this regard the situation is alarming. During the argumentation over the draft "fundamental law" for the Church one heard, for example: "What on earth are you worried about? No reasonable man any longer takes any notice of what comes from Rome!" The will to absolute government is certainly largely ineffective today, but it is also destructive of the church community.

2. This question is closely bound up with another: that of freedom and humanity in the Church. Whatever may be said about the Christian roots of our understanding of freedom and humanity, it is a fact that man in Western civilization has in the last two hundred years developed a specific feeling for these values without any contribution from the Church. It is a fact that for many men in situations of extreme unfreedom, the Church represents the hope of freedom and humanity, but it is also a fact that it far too often features that which contradicts these values as they are understood today. A laborious process of change is under way. But so long as "freedom" and "humanity" are not associated with the word "Church", the Church not only has no missionary future but falls under the judgment of the very Gospel of Jesus Christ that it preaches.

3. To resolve these problems, and to remain "loyal to its commission", may seem as difficult to the Church as squaring a circle. This is true in so far as there is no pre-eminent adequate answer to the problem. The claim to have one always leads to

totalitarianism. Therefore the Church today must also acknowledge a certain pluralism in its own regard: a readiness to "peace
and concord", even with members and constituent churches
which cannot simply be reduced to a common denominator in
wanting to remain in the service of the one Church of Christ and
its mission.

Pluralism does not mean just a bit of tolerance. Under certain
circumstances it must, within certain limits, affect the structural
unity of the Church. But, here as in other points, there is a desire
to preserve what one no longer has, and therefore a tendency to
lose what is urgently needed.

4. Compared with these basic questions of structural reform
of the Church, the technical problems of an efficient "administrative structure" are mild and of secondary importance. Ecclesiastical organisms will attain to a superhuman perfection as little
as any other bodies. Yet that cannot be any excuse for blocking
urgent administrative reforms on a basis of ideologized immobilism.

5. The existential form of the Church as a community is also
bound up with the structure of the Church. The process of restructuring is under way. The simple schema of parish—diocese
—world-Church has been upset in many ways. The Church now
exists in many different groups instead of and apart from the
"parish". The simple parallel division of offices (parish—parish
priest; diocese—bishop) often no longer corresponds to the facts.
In actual church life, the demarcation line runs between priests
and laity and more between ecclesiastically active and ecclesiastically passive baptized members. These are developments
which cannot be subsumed under a schema, but simply have to
be guided towards the best outcomes.

6. Finally, there is the question of the position of the Church
in society. The Church has become a minority social group. Many
of its structures and behaviour patterns, however, still derive
from the time when it enjoyed a majority position. The status of
minority group means a reduction of power, and means freedom.
In society the Church can only carry through what it can con-
vince people of. It is no longer in a position to apply pressures.
But it is also free, and must no longer support the powers and
forces which support it; it can speak its prophetic word to society.

The prophets of the Church seem to oscillate between hyper-criticism and hypersolidarization. But there is a sort of light dawning today in the fact that representatives of the Church are persecuted by the powerful precisely because they stand up for freedom and human dignity. This wins more credibility and future for the Church than "circumspect restraint, lest the activity of the Church is endangered". What activity—when things have come so far?

*   *   *

The rudiments for tackling all the reforms requisite in the Church today are already present. It is now a question of selection, in order to decide what is needed for the morrow; what is to be done away with in the present set-up; what faulty products are to be rejected; and what new approaches have to be developed. This is a process of selection that a "Third Vatican Council" could not undertake. It is a long process which must occur throughout the organism of the Church. Every member of the Church must be able to make his contribution; every one must fulfil his appropriate function. All have *one* Lord; and in all there operates the *one* Spirit, who distributes his gifts as he chooses.

Translated by John Griffiths

Adolf Exeler

Change of Consciousness and Church Reform

THERE is no single line of investigation along which to look for a solution of the set of problems considered in this article. At first sight the title might suggest the following question: "How can the realization of the need for church reform acquired by the theologians and perhaps also by church leaders be made in a real way the possession of the Church as a whole?" This is only one element in this set of problems, though its importance is such that I shall consider it first.

1. An effective reform cannot be carried out without the formation of an appropriate consciousness among all those involved. This is not true only of the Church. It has been found, for example, that slum clearance plans were unsuccessful until the authorities were able to inform the slum-dwellers at so early a stage, and involve them so closely in the planning, that they were able to identify with the operation and collaborate in working out the details. Reforms imposed by decree and not made intelligible are rarely effective. Recognition of this general truth allows us to see the immense importance of adult education in theology for the life of the Church. Among its other tasks, it must help to transmit the views on necessary reforms which have developed among theological specialists and church leaders effectively enough to allow at least the active part of the laity to consider them and express its opinion on them. When reforms are put into effect before the necessary change of consciousness has taken place they may very well produce the opposite effect to that intended. An example of this is the training and

appointment of large numbers of catechists in mission territories with a shortage of priests, which was at first rapturously received as the activation of the lay element in church life, but in practice often only strengthened the existing consumer mentality; only too frequently all those involved lacked the one thing necessary, an openness to the basic idea that in any community worthy of the name all the members are in principle called to take an active part in the work of the community.

In general one can say that the more intensive the efforts made in the general formation of consciousness, the more energetic can be the implementation of the necessary reforms. In this connection, those forms of theological adult education developed in a particular situation are particularly important. It is certainly not sufficient for the effective formation of consciousness to make use of the mass media, press, radio and television.[1] The importance of the mass media for the transformation of consciousness has been overestimated for a considerable time. It used to be thought that the individual was exposed to the influence of the media without any defence, that he was nothing more than a helpless consumer. More recent research into the media has drastically altered these views. It has shown that it is rarely possible to get people to change their attitudes through the use of the mass media alone. Closer investigation has indicated that for the process of consciousness and opinion formation the interpersonal network of communication is much more important. The decisive influences in the process are exercised by the people with whom one lives in close daily contact, family, friends, workmates, regular visitors. A person's most important views are normally formed over a period in the circle of such small groups. Small groups have a tendency to impose a screen between themselves and public opinion and its institutions, usually under the leadership of one member who is informally acknowledged as the leader of the group and can be called the "leader of opinion". It seems that this attitude is stronger now than in the past, and that a defence mechanism is operating in response to the excessive demands of the wide range of views put forward in public

[1] For the whole of the following paragraph, cf. Elmar Bartsch *et al.*, *Verkündigung* (Mainz, 1970), pp. 25 f.

discussion. The individual is exposed to so many value systems, models of behaviour and appeals that, in order not to be reduced to impotence by the multiplicity of possibilities offered, he takes up a critical distance from them all, and his decision, which usually involves a compromise between the various demands, is taken within the framework of the small group which is most important to him. Theological adult education can be effective only to the extent that it is in contact with these small groups. In order to have effective contact it must adapt itself as far as possible to the vocabulary and ways of thought and argument of the people to whom it is directed.

These considerations show why small discussion and action groups are much more important than sermons and lectures. Action is particularly effective when such a group tackles a specific problem which directly concerns them and thus forms a sort of task force.

Where there is a feeling that winning the support of the people for intended reforms is unimportant, important objectives of the reforms are threatened at the start. Since people are not easily moved from familiar views, and since such people generally form close relations with others who hold similar views, it would be a mistake to imagine that it is a simple matter to provide the necessary information to justify a reform. A whole range of psychological factors make it difficult for the individual to reorient himself to new attitudes and ideas. With most people, intellectual as well as physical mobility declines with age. This is not a biological law but a fact resulting from a lack of training in adapting to new ideas, or from the absence of opportunities for adult education. This generally observable reluctance to accept new ways of thought is considerably strengthened in matters connected with the Church by the widespread encouragement of an attitude of immobilism. To the degree that the church system till now seemed to be governed by immutable norms, an expectation of changing ("converting") others, but not oneself, was encouraged. (It is significant that when the members of the various churches speak of "converts" they do not mean themselves, but others, who previously belonged to another church.) It used to be possible to regard oneself as a staunch Christian just because one was willing to adopt a particular new idea. This attitude was reinforced by a dogmatic theology and canon law which seemed to allow no more than peripheral changes.

More recently, everyone has become accustomed to living in a dynamic society which is involved in a constant process of transformation. Rapid and lasting transformations in almost every area of life have required an appropriate change in consciousness. For this reason, training for an informed and responsible manœuvrability has become a basic educational task. It is not always easy to carry out because the constant obligation to adapt to new situations is much more often felt as a burden than a relief. Nevertheless, most of our contemporaries have become accustomed to the idea that constant changes are unavoidable in the sphere of technology, but there is no automatic transfer from this experience to religious life. On the contrary, it makes many people all the more anxious to be "left in peace" in this one sphere of religion. Who, after all, can tolerate constant challenging of his assumptions? Even in the case of many of those who for many years regarded themselves as progressive, and indeed were, there is in the course of time a decrease in the energy necessary to take up new attitudes and consequently also in openness to new ways of thought. They jib, because it is more than they can manage to be obliged constantly to re-think everything afresh at an ever-increasing rate.

All this indicates not only the great importance of theological adult education, but also the great number of difficulties it faces. And the difficulties seem all the greater when one realizes that our considerations so far have gone in only one direction and are far from adequate to deal with the complexity of the situation. If we wish to do justice to the situation, quite different aspects must be taken into consideration and very different perspectives adopted.

2. We have looked at the need for a change of consciousness among church members if church reform is to be effectively implemented, but the converse is also true: the change in consciousness often precedes the plan for church reform. As a result of the constantly changing surroundings in which a person lives today, even within his restricted group, there is frequently a constant and often unnoticed change in consciousness. Many adults are amazed when, on investigation, they discover how far and

how radically their views in a number of areas have altered within a few years. This observation runs counter to the argument of the first section, but it would be a sign of ideological blindness not to accept it. It shows us why church reform almost always lags behind the general development of consciousness.

We must take into account, however, that the change in consciousness brought about by the immediate environment is more noticeable at the "base" than among the leadership or professional theologians. And not merely stronger; there is often a marked divergence between the church leadership and the "base" in this area. The danger of institutional blindness brought about by one's own involvement in the continuing and apparently normal fuctioning of the institution is much greater among church leaders than at the "grass-roots". Nor are professional theologians always the most sensitive to the changes required. It is safe to say that many very "progressive" theologians would be amazed to discover how little their laboriously worked out theories correspond to actual requirements. A parish priest or one active among young people feels much more directly the absence of response or the changed response to what was formerly held to be permanently valid, or the negative response to reforms suggested or imposed "from above". Such a priest will frequently have to break away from official patterns of behaviour in order to be able to speak with his people at all. This dependence on response is felt much more directly at the "grass-roots" than at high-level meetings or in theology lecture-rooms. The youth chaplain, for example, cannot avoid experimenting to see what actually "works". It would be a complete misunderstanding to dismiss such experiments as following fashion, lack of firmness or disloyalty to the faith. Deliberate experimentation may well be intended to make contact with new growth points for a development of a consciousness of faith in the future which appear "from below". Many fruitful starting-points for church reform have appeared in this way in the course of history, often even in the form of constructive disobedience. In these situations there were no rules and no completely worked out theory, merely a very strong feeling of the practical necessity to do something in a different way from before. This applies not only in the field of liturgy, but also to the pastoral treatment of (say) mixed marriages or divorced and remarried Catholics; it even extends to the verbal expression of the consciousness of faith.

When a difference appears between the official faith of the Church and the actual faith of the faithful, this should not automatically be regarded as a reason for blaming the faithful. We should at least allow for the possibility that these are not simply symptoms of decline but new impulses containing the promise of valid innovations.

In all this, the position of young people is most important. Young people are naturally inclined to iconoclasm[2] with regard to the established forms of church life, as to other things; they refuse to take over uncritically what has hitherto been regarded as beyond question. They try to develop new life-styles and new forms of thought and action, and this holds also for the faith. Those who are concerned about genuine church reform would be wise to pay careful attention to the new elements which emerge among the young. (In this connection a phenomenon such as the "youth council" at Taizé deserves particular attention.) Where a change of consciousness leads to a critical judgment on what was previously accepted as valid but does not go on to produce the change recognized as necessary, tensions and frustrations are inevitable. These can become so strong that interest in reform turns into a complete abandonment of participation. Even theology students often drift away as a result of disappointment. They drift into anti-authoritarian movements, where they hope to find what they looked for in vain in the Church, or they adopt orthodox Marxism: having got free of one form of orthodoxy they immediately end up in another. In less professedly oppositional movements there is a tendency towards the disciplines which have as their objective the change which theology no longer seems able to offer: i.e., educational theory, psychology and sociology.

3. The great objection to a properly prepared effort to bring about a change of consciousness is the demand that one must take care of "the weak". We may well ask, however, whether possibly the widespread "confusion" among the "simple faithful"

[2] Cf. Hugo Assmann, "Theologie der Revolution als Sprach-Ikonoklasmus und neues Sprechen", in Ernst Feil/Rudolf Weth, *Diskussion zur "Theologie der Revolution"* (Munich and Mainz, 1969), pp. 235-40.

is not rather the result of a lack of explanation and information than of an excess; may not the responsibility for such confusion rest with the serious deficit of information which is at least in part due to the filtering of information still so frequent in the Church?[3] The *sensus ecclesiae* is not automatically present in greater measure where there has so far been passive acceptance of existing rules; this can be seen particularly clearly from the reform movements of the past, initiated and led by saints. Of course, not every initiative for reform today can be justified by an appeal to these historical phenomena, but even less can a nervous hostility to every reform and any change of consciousness be maintained on historical grounds.

4. The points already discussed point to the conclusion that a complex learning process is required if we are to have effective reform in the Church, yet we are still far from having considered all the aspects of the problems involved. We must take account of the fact that it is possible for a considerable change in consciousness to be brought about through the experience of an imposed reform. To take only one example, repeated participation in ecumenical marriage services can radically alter a previously rigid opposition to mixed marriages. At any rate, there is a complex interplay between the various factors. In order to meet the needs of the situation we must think in terms of some form of group decision-making, and be careful in practice to allow the group to function. Programmes which are drawn up "from above" need feed-back from the base, and there must be room for this to include not just corrections on minor points but basic innovations. Various attempts in German dioceses in connection with the regional planning of the Church show how such group decision-making could function. In the diocese of Münster a "structural plan" was presented "from above" in 1969. After vigorous discussion at the base it had to be shelved because it was not accepted. On the other hand, in the archdiocese of Freiburg a different approach was chosen. All that came "from above" were some general suggestions for the discussion of the subject, with the request that suggestions for the reorganization of the church's territorial structures should be worked out "from

[3] Cf. J. B. Metz, *Reform und Gegenreformation heute* (Mainz, 1969), pp. 21 f.

below". The suggestions this method produced were criticized and developed by experts, with the result that within two years such a change of consciousness had taken place among both priests and parish councils that the necessary forms were not merely requested but asked for.

This sort of group decision-making indicates the task of a practical theology concerned with the future. It must have a strong empirical emphasis, and in this area should proceed in a similar way to the curriculum research which has been carried out in Germany for some time under Anglo-American influence. Curriculum research has abandoned *a priori* and arbitrary procedures, and tries to develop group decision-making, on the general assumption that the investigation of individual factors and the views and experiences of the "clients" have an effect on each other. If we were to transfer this approach to practical theology, it would imply the task of using empirical methods not simply to give prominence to current views but above all to detect long-term trends. Theological adult education in this context could no longer have the function of transmitting information only from "above" to "below", but also in the opposite direction. The appropriate methods for this still have to be developed. If theological adult education wants not only to "get across" what others have worked out, but to stimulate processes of thought which will allow a flow of information in both directions, it must bring to consciousness the connections I have described. Among methods which could be used are role playing (where one puts oneself into the place of someone else, a bishop, a theologian, a parish priest, or a conservative or progressive member of the Church); group dynamics, the examination of aggressive behaviour so that people learn to listen to others, the description of experiences against the background of people's own accounts of their different situations; and many others. It is now possible to see many hitherto largely neglected dimensions of theological adult education. Such an approach assumes that training for intellectual flexibility will be one of the chief tasks of religious education. When a Christian begins to think that he has already reached full maturity in his faith, his intellectual powers are getting slack. He sees his main task as defending what has been achieved, whereas he should really be concentrating on what could not be achieved until now.[4] The goal of a concern with questions of faith is not an orthodoxy without questions, but a permanent intellectual openness. What some people regard as orthodoxy is simply the result of mental laziness, while what some people regard as vacillation is simply a constant readiness to change. Intellectual openness and a capacity for change should not, however, remain "intellectual" accomplishments, reserved to a few individuals or restricted groups; this would lead to frustration and loss of interest. These qualities call also for a reform of the whole life of the Church which will show it to be capable of change and open to the future, to be a community which, in spite of its realization that it is by definition irredeemably transitory, must constantly transcend its practical inadequacy as an expression of its hope for what it can never achieve on its own.

[4] Cf. Otto Betz, *Die Zumutung des Glaubens* (Munich, 1968), pp. 60 f., 91.

Translated by Francis McDonagh

Adrian Hastings

Should Church Reform start from the Top or from Ground Level?

IN attempting a reply to this question it is useful to begin by considering the recent process of conciliar reform in itself. Many of the major reforms of Vatican II, as is clear from a study of the first drafts, were hardly desired or intended by those planning it at the centre. Yet the Council agreed upon great reforms, some of which are still in process of implementation, and set the stage for others which are now being fought over; what was done could not have been done without the action of central authority and its authorization. This was largely so, of course, because central authority has had a tremendous blocking power, a power of veto, in the Catholic Church: its negative can be far more effective than its positive force. So a decision at the centre to withdraw the veto was necessary for reform, though positively it is far less effective in implementing it.

It is equally true that the reforms of the Council were mostly not previously desired outside the centre by the majority of the hierarchy, nor by a majority of priests, nor even consciously in most places by the laity. They have subsequently been implemented to a very considerable extent, partly because of the weight of authority at the top, but still more because of the contagion of example spreading from one local church to another. Though it would be a great over-simplification to say that post-conciliar reform has been reform from the centre, yet the centre has made it possible, both by the withdrawal of the veto in various areas and by the provision of general norms. The attitude of docility to Rome remains so strong in senior hierarchs and among the

87

people generally that they have quite rapidly carried out measures to which they were temperamentally opposed, had explicitly resisted for many years, and had hardly now been converted to in their hearts: such is still the strength of discipline within the Roman Catholic communion. The speed of reform and change in attitudes has indeed amazed many non-Catholic observers. On a first view, reform by conciliar and papal instruction appears remarkably effective. It is important then to examine the inherent limitations in such reform from the top.

As a matter of fact, the most significant reforms of the Council were approved not because of a previous majority for them nor because of papal backing, but rather because of the effective and convincing dynamism of a minority who had previously seen the need and now at last had a more or less satisfactory forum: this dynamic group, a relatively small number of bishops and their supporting theologians, came principally from a rather limited number of local churches. A widespread sympathy for *aggiornamento*, fostered by Pope John himself, was gradually transformed through the advocacy of a minority into an overwhelming ecclesial consensus. This could only have been done, at least with this sort of rapidity, in a context such as central authority and a general council could provide. In this way the Council operated as a mechanism of release enabling the new vision and dynamism working in some local churches to influence many others rather quickly. The vision had not come from the top, but it needed the top as a channel of effective communication.

The use of the mechanisms of the highest authority to get reform started, and even dialogue for reform, was particularly necessary at the end of the 1950s just because freedom of speech had been for some time so very much restricted within the Church. In the freer and more permissive atmosphere of the late 1960s it has certainly been far easier for an ecclesial consensus to develop, as for regional movements of reform to spread effectively, without the same degree of intervention from the top, or even despite such intervention. Vatican II has in fact generated a church atmosphere of freedom, dialogue, consciousness of the local church and of the need for change, which makes possible mechanisms of reform somewhat different from those which, with regard to the Church as a whole, were necessary ten years ago to get anything started at all.

The Council itself, moreover, while initially thinking in terms of reform of the Church as a whole, and indeed continuing so to think, was progressively constrained to discard the preconception that a uniform solution could be offered to problems in almost any field. The diversity of situation between local churches and socio-economic areas made the attempt at monolithic reform self-contradictory. Sheer practical necessity enforced the rediscovery of the theology of the local church: the *ecclesia particularis*, the smaller ecclesial unit with its own characteristic needs and the power to respond to them. Such a staggering statement (in the context of the Roman tradition) could even be made as that the Council "solemnly declares that the churches of the East, as much as those of the West, fully enjoy the right, and are in duty bound, to rule themselves" (*Decree on Eastern Catholic Churches*, a. 5). The churches of the West, one might add, as much as those of the East. However, neither the theological nor the practical implications of such a statement were adequately realized in the atmosphere of the Council, nor subsequently by the post-conciliar curia; much of the frustration in recent reform has come about as a result.

It is becoming ever clearer that reform can only be valid and effective when it is a response to the needs and opportunities of a local church; this is true whether it be reform of the *koinonia*, the communion with its structures of fellowship and ministry; whether it be reform of the *kerygma*, the message for today, its theological interpretation and catechesis; whether it be reform of the *diakonia*, the temporal service which finds man in his needs here and now; or whether it be reform of the *leiturgia*, the explicit worship of the believing community.

Within each field and between each field there are questions of priority, of where here and now to direct one's reforming efforts: to concentrate upon liturgy in a racially torn country may be to betray the *diakonia*, to work up an intensity of feeling about racialism in Sweden may be a betrayal of the *kerygma*. Next, there are questions as to the shape of the reform needed, and there are questions of timing. As regards the latter, there is within a movement of reform an ideal moment when men are ready for much, but which, if it is not seized, can quickly pass and obstinately fail to return. Such a moment is often proper to a local situation. This is particularly true in the area of ecumenism and any system of insisting upon a more or less uniform speed of advance at world level will effectively prevent response to it. If the moment is not seized, an essential element of sincerity is lost, the movement becomes flabby and ceases to be quite genuine.

In the field of liturgical reform two strategies have clearly emerged since the Council. On one side is the official strategy, the reform of something which one still persists in calling "the Latin Rite". This envisages a decisive continuing liturgical unity to be determined in Rome apart from a few marginal details left to local discretion. This goes so far as to require the sending to Rome for approval of texts of liturgical translations into languages which not a single person in Rome is able to read. After several months they are duly returned as authorized. On the other side is the strategy which holds that the maintenance within the liturgical unity of the "Latin Rite" of countries so vastly disparate as Ceylon, New Zealand, Tanzania, Peru and Norway on the grounds that they all together form "the Western Church" is pastorally undesirable, and theologically a denial of any sense beyond the antiquarian in a recognition of the autonomy of the "Eastern churches" themselves.

No one should doubt that the adoption of the principles of the vernacular and of integral popular participation have greatly benefited the Church everywhere. Nevertheless, to a very considerable extent, the liturgical reforms of the last few years can be seen as the imposition of a pattern of worship judged suitable for modern Western Europe and North America upon the whole world regardless of a real impoverishment in worshipping life that this has entailed for people whose social and cultural attitudes are strongly different from those of the West. Compare the Western situation to that of rural Africa. It has been a chief aim of the modern liturgical movement to make liturgy "relevant" to a society which is largely urban, industrial, literate and scientifically minded. It has to be made helpful to people who live in large urban complexes, who hardly know the people in the same street, who are in a hurry with trains to catch, and so forth. In most parts of Africa, however, the great majority of people are rural, they are not in such a hurry, they live in small villages, they know all their neighbours, they read little or nothing, they are not scientifically minded.

The new liturgy is becoming more and more cerebral, so many outward signs and picturesque ceremonies have been removed. One even senses in some quarters a certain contempt for ritual in itself. An educated society may want a cerebral liturgy, something appealing very directly to the brain, but an uneducated people want a sensible liturgy, something with plenty of symbolism, a rich ritual with varied action and repetitive singing. As to length, it is perfectly clear that many of the liturgical reforms are designed to make ceremonies rather brief, to cut duplication. In the rush and hurry of life in the Western world this may be desirable, there is so much else to do, attention cannot be held for long. In the country there is not so much else, people may have walked miles to come to church, they have no television to return to, they want a good show not a skimped ceremony. Again, understanding is necessary wherever one is, but understanding can take different forms. The Western stress today is predominantly upon verbal understanding of every word and phrase used: it is the sort of understanding taught in secondary schools. Largely illiterate people do not look for that. What they seek is a global understanding of what the thing is all about. Sensing the symbolism of an action may be far more important and significant than following every phrase the priest uses. The contrasts here go very deep and could be much developed, but they do show how misadvised is the attempt to reform the liturgy in a more or less uniform manner for the whole world.

If we turn again to the *diakonia* of the Church: the service of human society in terms of development and secular liberation. If the vitality of the Church's fellowship and the fruitfulness of its *kerygma* need always to be manifested in the sincerity and effectiveness of its *diakonia*, this has to be done in very different ways in affluent and third-world countries, in lands ruled by Communists and lands ruled by racialists, in lands where a large proportion of the population are Christian and lands where the Church is a tiny minority, in lands where in the past the Church has been closely linked with structures of exploitation and lands where it has not. A blanket concern for "development" directed, maybe, by a centralized "Justice and Peace Commission" could be truly disastrous from the viewpoint of a true reform of the Church's relationship to secular needs and structures. Only the local church can finally judge of its own local *diakonia* or indeed how it should participate, as it must do, in a wider *diakonia*. This is well recognized in Pope Paul's letter on the subject to Cardinal Léger, dated 14 May 1971. Yet, here as elsewhere, the local church and local reform cannot be left without the stimulus and even the judgment of the wider communion. Its failure can produce a counter-sign of more than local dimensions. The secular *diakonia* of each local church is today inextricably interwoven with the widest Catholic witness and its reform may need to be triggered off not only at local but at world level.

Ecumenism, the reform of the Church as wrongly divided, is again something which can certainly not be envisaged in merely local terms and yet which will surely only be very partially effective if it is largely controlled from the centre. The needs and possibilities in diverse areas are so profoundly different. This difference relates to a number of vital factors: firstly, there is the contrast between a region where the great majority of people are either nominally Christians or have descended from Christians and a region where all the Christians together may form five, ten or twenty per cent of the population, living amid and witnessing to a vast committed majority of Moslems, Hindus or Buddhists. Secondly, there is the difference created by the numerical balance between Catholics and other Christians. The approach in lands where Catholics form a great majority, and have perhaps a past tradition of oppressing their separated brethren, cannot be the same as that in places where there is a certain balance between communions, or again where Catholics are very few. Thirdly, there is the factor of the character of the chief separated group with which Catholics are here in contact: pre-Chalcedonian Easterners, Greeks, "High Church" Anglicans, Evangelical Anglicans, Lutherans, Baptists, and so forth. There is a great danger that the Ecumenical Directory and the tendency to play safe in quite different real situations by clinging to its norms in practice provide a way of behaving here and now very inappropriate for a great number of situations. Fourthly, there is the degree of local division and the balance within the non-Catholic Christian community. There has in practice to be an order of priorities in inter-communion schemes for greater unity. Where there is a great diversity among Protestants, ecumenical priorities may indicate a certain holding back in regard to Catholic-Protestant relations by churches which react differently in other situations where Protestant disunity is not so apparent or has already been overcome. Fifthly, there is the amount which has already been achieved in a particular country. Some places began very much earlier and are now far further on the road than are others. A norm which here and now may appear extremely bold in one area may seem positively retrogressive in another. Such is the complexity of Christian division that the hopes of real reunion get smaller the more they are related to a world-wide achievement rather than to a local one. The theological issue here is very delicate. The re-establishment of full communion, whose horizons are essentially catholic, cannot finally be envisaged in merely local terms, nevertheless much more local freedom is necessary and today there is in fact a continual tension between a Rome directed ecumenism on the one hand and the varied possibilities throughout the world upon the other.

In the field of structural reform it is again clear how vastly the needs of different local churches vary. The almost universal cry of a "shortage of priestly vocations" (but not in South India) should not blind one to the fact that the existing situation, the coming needs and the ways in which they can possibly be met, are all different. Thus a shortage of vocations means one thing in Holland and quite another in Chile, because the whole background of the Church and existing priest/laity ratios are so different. The structural needs of any one group of churches must not be judged in terms proper to those of another. Thus in most parts of Africa (as of South America) the number of ordinations is and has long been pitifully small, but the existence of tens of thousands of married catechists—some of whom have had a training course of two years or more—presents (as in Asia, but not elsewhere) a highly important existing structural element lacking in many other more developed churches.

Any attempt to lay down from the centre a single pattern of structural reform for the whole Church could not possibly succeed. It would not really be practical even within a single area. Take Eastern Africa, for example, and three dioceses within it: Ndola, Kigoma and Masaka. Ndola diocese in Zambia includes the copperbelt; it is a relatively wealthy, predominantly urban society with towards a million people, perhaps thirty per cent of whom would claim to be Catholics. It has in all some seven local priests and hardly any seminarians. It has also very few catechists, but many fairly well-educated lay Catholics in well-paid employment. Kigoma in Tanzania is a quickly growing young diocese with over 80,000 Catholics covering an extensive, poor and wholly rural area with some three local priests but many catechists, some rather well trained. Masaka diocese in Uganda is a relatively small, fairly prosperous and densely populated area with some 300,000 Catholics (over half the total population), about a hundred local priests (many of them rather old) and a large number of catechists who have either no training or very little. Listing other dioceses one could continue to ring the changes, though the pattern of Kigoma is more characteristic of Africa as a whole than that of Masaka or Ndola. Sound reform of the ministry must start with the present position, making use of existing resources, not distressing those who are already trying to do the job, and so forth. The needs and opportunities of Ndola, Kigoma and Masaka are obviously strikingly diverse and could not be properly tackled with a single formula, yet all have a very strong need for structural reform of one kind or another.

The guidance of a "Directory" can often help us little with the true business of effective reform, indeed it may even obscure the real problems and needs of a particular area by identifying the reform proper for a certain ecclesial or cultural area with reform as such and by diverting the limited energies of well-intentioned reformers into tackling what in their own local context are really pseudo-problems.

Yet it remains true in the post-conciliar world that some local hierarchies, clergies and people remain psychologically so Rome-orientated, and so uniformity-orientated, that they may do next to nothing if they are not clearly directed by Rome. Hence, as a matter of fact, it is true that in some areas if there is not reform almost imposed from the centre, there may still be no reform. In the field of ecumenism, for instance, it is still the case in some parts that Rome-inspired efforts have as alternative almost no efforts at all or (perhaps) efforts by a few people effectively vetoed by the authority of the hierarchy. For at the level of the national hierarchy, just as at that of the universal Church, the effective power of higher authority is rather one of veto than one of positive action.

The Catholic Church is necessarily a subtle balance of local church and universal communion; its continual reform, being an integral element in its healthy life, has to share in this balance. It is most necessary that local churches should be open to the influence of the whole and of the centre, and there are decisions of living as well as of believing which are fittingly taken at a universal level, and so it has always been. Local churches must not be in bondage to the world Church and to the see of unity (though such has for long been nearly the case), but they must not be mentally schismatic either, unwilling to accept a wider consensus, a call for reform or a ruling from the apostolic college or its head. There needs to be a continual give and take, in which initiatives come most frequently from below but the ruling of conflicts and the decisive fiat to change major pieces of existing discipline come from above.

There are indeed decisions which need to be taken at world level, both because of the nature of the Catholic Church and because of the increasingly inter-involved character of modern world society. The very sharing of problems by local churches at the level of the *Catholica* generates a deeper sense of their meaning, greater determination to resolve them, and at the same time builds up the reality of catholic communion. Reform cannot be purely local and a determination to make it so would truly be schismatic. The world Church has to influence local churches, and perhaps trigger off their self-questioning. Equally, local churches must influence each other, from parish to parish, diocese to diocese, and national church to national church. Of its nature, the contagion of reform spreads from one to another, but has continually to be adapted in the process—the unadapted adoption of Dutch reform or American reform in India or the Congo is just as wrong as the adoption of "Roman" reform. In most things the decisive pastoral judgment has to be a local one, and the final effectiveness of any reform has never depended upon Pope or

Council but upon the zeal, contemporary faith, and sense of realistic adaptation of the local ministry and Christian community.

Finally and supremely, reform is super-eminently the work of the Holy Spirit: the renewal in life with which above all we associate him. He is present in all living members of the Church, in those "above" as in those "below". He is above the one, below the other, and breathes where he will. He may grant the charism of a reformer to a Catherine of Siena or to a John XXIII, to a Vincent Lebbe, a Francis of Assisi or a Cardinal Bea. It may be a village catechist one time, an archbishop and chairman of an episcopal conference the next. The charism of the reformer is an almost infinitely varied one and in a Spirit-guided Church we cannot say where it is next to be found. But where the spirit is, there will be the body—the structural shape of a particular reform will depend to no inconsiderable degree on the position within the Church of the one who has this time been given the outstanding charism. One time the vision, the dynamism, the new creation may issue from the lowest of grass roots; another time from the chair of Peter. We can only respect the freedom of the Spirit, but we can be sure too that he will respect the dynamics of human society and the diversity of our predicament within the *ecclesia ecclesiarum.*

Peter Huizing

Comments on the Revision of Canon Law

The Pope's Address to Canonists

ON 20 January 1970, the Pope addressed a congress on canon law organized by the University of Rome. He stressed the duty of canon lawyers to look carefully in Scripture and tradition for the origins of their science in view of the deeper understanding of the inner reality of the Church brought to light by the Second Vatican Council. He said that the age-old practice of basing canonical teaching on an undisputed legal tradition was no longer possible. Nor could canonists continue to reinforce their teaching with elements taken firstly from Roman law—their *ratio scripta* or "written reason"—and later from the law of those people who had Christianity preached to them. They would, of course, have to continue to some extent to do this, but at the same time they were obliged now to look for the "why" and the "how" of canon law in the mystical constitution of the Church itself.

The Pope believed that it was on these principles that the renewed study and formulation of the Church's law had to be based and that the revision of the existing code of canon law would result from this renewal. This revision was not necessary mainly for practical reasons, although this had almost always been the case with collections of canon law in the past. It was, on the contrary, necessary because the Church's law had to be derived from the very essence and being of the Church itself. What had, in other words, to be expressed above all in the external order of the Church was the evangelical law of love and of the grace of the Holy Spirit, the inward principle of all activity in the Church. The Pope observed, however, that it was easier at present to anticipate all this in rather vague terms than to predict the consequences of this revision.[1]

A number of fundamental requirements for the revision of the Church's law in general, and of the codex in particular, were stated in this papal address. On the one hand, the Church cannot entirely ignore contemporary views concerning the organization of society in general and that of the maintenance of law in particular. On the other hand, however, in its own organization —one of the most striking aspects of its visible appearance—the Church has also to be a recognizable expression in its evangelical inspiration and its mission to the world. The question that we are bound to ask, then, is this. Can all these demands be satisfied by the method chosen for the revision of the code of canon law?

The Papal Commission

On 28 March 1963, Pope John XXIII set up a papal commission with the task of revising the codex. There are now about seventy members, all of them cardinals. The commission has met twice, on 25 November 1965 and on 28 May 1968, when some very general statements were made about an outline *Lex Ecclesiae Fundamentalis* and the systematic arrangement of the revised codex. The members of the commission were individually invited to send in their views concerning the draft *Lex Fundamentalis* and this was then sent to the bishops. Up till now, the commission has really been more of an honorary committee than an effective organ and it has not proved capable of exercising a real function in the work of revising canon law. It is indeed difficult to see how it can be effective.

The Advisers

There are now about a hundred and thirty advisers, as far as possible invited from all parts of the world. Most, though not all, are canonists. Five are laymen, but there are no women. The average age is rather more than middle age. They are divided into different study groups, each with its special subject. These

[1] *Acta Apostolicae Sedis* 62 (1970), 106-11.

include the systematic arrangement of the code of canon law, the *Lex Fundamentalis*, universal norms, the hierarchy, the institutions of perfection, the laity and associations of the faithful, persons and legal persons, marriage, the other sacraments, the Church's teaching office, the law of procedure and penal law. The point of departure chosen by most of these groups for their work of revision has been the text and order of the codex. The members of each group are expected to write a study of the subject of the next meeting and to send this in time to the secretariat. A *relator* or reporter sets the various suggestions that have been made in the different studies in order, perhaps even in the form of new *canones* or laws, and puts these forward for discussion in the assembly. Decisions are taken about the texts of schemes on agreement or on a majority of votes and mention is made in the minutes of dissenting opinions.

Information about the Work of the Advisers

Apart from the unofficial publication of the draft scheme of the *Lex Fundamentalis* which was sent to the bishops, very little information has been given about the work of the study groups. Since 1969, the commission has periodically published *Communicationes*, containing a certain amount of general information. I gave a brief survey of this in the October number of *Concilium* 1971.[2] Information is exchanged between the various study groups only when there is a close connection between questions arising in different groups. The minutes of the assemblies are passed on to the members of the groups and, although there is no formal pledge of secrecy, they are confidential. Information can, of course, be exchanged verbally, at the discretion of the members of the groups.

An Assessment of the Work done

A criticism of the *Lex Fundamentalis* has already appeared in *Concilium*.[3] What can be said about the rest of the work, in so far as it has been published in the *Communicationes*?

[2] P. Huizing, "The Revision of Canon Law", in *Concilium* 8 (1971), pp. 124-32 (American edn. Vol. 68).
[3] G. A. Bologna, "A Constitutional Law for the Church", *op. cit.*, pp. 135-50.

In the first place, it is a great pity that the information has been so scanty and so general. The president of the commission, Cardinal Felici, and the secretariat cannot be blamed for this. There is no official secrecy, but a real desire to furnish the more complete information which might result in expert criticism of the commission's work is frustrated by a simple lack of staff and means.

As far as can be judged from this incomplete information, there are many positive aspects of the work done so far. The study group for the laity and associations of the faithful has drawn up a statutory scheme outlining the rights and duties that are recognized as pertaining to every believer, lay or clerical, by necessity and not by virtue of recognition on the part of the Church's authority. The Church has the obligation to recognize these rights and duties and to protect the rights. The scheme then deals with a number of rights which apply particularly, or at least more particularly, to the laity. A clear advance on the existing code of canon law is made in the law concerning associations of the faithful, which is very general indeed and allows a great deal of freedom to the associations themselves, in their own statutory provisions.

The part of the code of canon law devoted to penal law has been considerably reduced in the scheme provided by this study group, which suggests that penal law should be restricted to the public sphere of life, so that confessors should no longer have to concern themselves with this aspect of the Church's law. As much attention as possible is given in this draft to pastoral needs, the dignity of the human person, and the protection of man's rights. The scheme stresses the principle that punishments should only be imposed if there is no other way of remedying the situation, and that it should only in very rare cases be possible to determine penalties incurred by a simple breach of the law (*poenae latae sententiae*). Relatively few offences are regarded as punishable. These are clearly improvements.

There are also many positive elements in the work of the group responsible for the *institutiones perfectionis*. It is proposed, for example, that only universally valid fundamental norms should be included in the codex, leaving the institutions themselves much greater freedom and that provisions determining the government of the institutions should express the conciliar ideal of co-operation between all members. Finally, no distinction is made between institutions for men and those for women.

The revision of the law of procedure also tries to ensure that the rights of the individual believer are fully protected, and special rules have been set out governing administrative procedure, that is, jurisdiction concerning disputes about acts of government when an individual believes that his rights have been violated.

Objections to the Work done

Despite the many positive aspects contained in the suggestions that have already been published, there are many dubious elements, especially with regard to the ultimate value and the practical application of the work done. Let me illustrate what I mean by a few examples.

There are legal restrictions in the statutory provisions regarding the faithful and the laity which have no place in statutory law. If such restrictions are included in the definition of the law, then the law itself is practically whittled away, even though this may be unintentional. Lay people are, for example, given the right to express their opinions publicly about church affairs, *provided* that they respect the Church's magisterium, and provided that they have the necessary expert knowledge. This means in practice that their right is restricted to the expression of respectful, expert opinions. In other words, the ethical conditions for a morally justified use of rights are made the content of the law itself. The authority which has to decide about the exercise of these rights or the judge who has to make a pronouncement might therefore be able to deny the existence of such rights because they do not show the necessary respect for authority or the necessary expert knowledge. The law ought to include legal provisions regarding liability for the misuse of rights, but it should not make the content of laws dependent on the ethically justified use of those laws. Such restrictions should, in that case, have to be included in all rights, not only those pertaining to lay people, but also those relating to the Pope and the bishops, who should also have to exercise their rights with the necessary respect for all believers and with the necessary expert knowledge and so on.

The basic laws concerning the faithful contain one law according to which there should be no penalty except for transgressions defined by the law and, in that case, the punishment should be determined by the same law. There is no mention in the report issued by the group in charge of the revision of penal law of any such provision. I am of the opinion that this kind of provision has a place in civil law, but not in the statutory laws of the Church. In the Church, a person ought to be certain that he will be judged justly. He ought not to be certain that a judgment can only apply to him when he has committed an offence that has been previously defined. The Church, on the other hand, should be free to disapprove publicly of actions which are strictly speaking not within its jurisdiction. Canon law ought to be able to offer protection against any indiscriminate judgments, but not to provide certainties about what is really the province of civil law.

Although considerable reductions have been suggested in the penal law of the Church, nothing essential has been eliminated from the system itself. There are still *poenae latae sententiae*. There are still penalties which embrace a whole series of punishments such as excommunication and suspension. There is still the situation where a judge imposes punishments or declares that someone has incurred penalties *latae sententiae*, although judges have not in fact done this in the Church in living memory. It is also very questionable whether the proposal to introduce an administration of penal justice into canon law will ever succeed in practice. Another provision which raises far-reaching questions with regard to the new law as a whole is that Christians who were not baptized in the Catholic Church do not come within the law unless a provision determines otherwise.

In the section on the religious communities, the code of canon law dealt only with institutions with public vows. After this, it dealt with institutions without such vows but with a communal life. It was a happy inspiration on the part of the study group to introduce one name under which all the institutions could be included, but the name chosen for these institutions set up by the Church, and consisting of members joined together in a resolution to keep the evangelical counsels, was less fortunate. This group took as its principle the fact that the laws of the Church should be expressed in such a way as to encourage vocations and to provide support for the religious life and protection against the dangers that might threaten it. At the same time, however, it had to be made quite clear that the keeping of canon law alone did not constitute a perfect religious life. This resulted in scriptural and theological texts (precisely what these texts are is not known) being included in the scheme together with strictly legal provisions. One wonders whether a mixture of canonical provisions and scriptural and theological texts will not have precisely the opposite effect, in other words, whether all these elements will not be treated in the same way and all be in danger of being given the same degree of importance as scriptural texts.

As far as can be ascertained from the information available, no essential changes have been made in the law of procedure. The most important new element is administrative procedure, but it is hardly surprising that a certain amount of scepticism exists regarding the practical introduction of this aspect into the codex. The somewhat simplified procedure to be used in matrimonial cases can only be regarded as a tentative beginning. The really urgent problems of marriage cases which stand in the way of a realistic pastoral approach are nowhere near a solution.

The Habit of Canonists

Most of the advisers in the study groups are canon lawyers, either with long experience in the practical application of canon law in papal or episcopal courts or offices or with years of study and teaching behind them. These men are now asked to reconsider the whole of their teaching in the light of the conciliar statements about the Church and of recent scriptural and theological thinking. Then, in his address of 20 January 1970, the Pope referred to the importance of a *Lex Fundamentalis* in the Church and was clearly of the opinion that the whole of canon law had to be revised in the light of this constitutional law. One might even go so far as to say that the most competent canonists and those with the most experience are the least suitable for this task. How can we be expected to give up our life-long habit of basing our teaching on an undisputed tradition that is centuries old?

It is very difficult indeed for us to deny the truth of axioms that we have defended all our lives as the basic principles of canon law, even if we are told that they are disputed or even denied by theologians. If we are told that exegetes, Church historians and theologians are now teaching different doctrines concerning Christian marriage and its indissolubility, different from what we were taught in the seminary, we tend to fear heresy because we can only think about marriage and the indissolubility of marriage within the framework of canon law. We cannot entertain doubts as to whether a penal law is not opportune in the Church, because we were taught that the Church was a perfect society and every perfect society must have a penal law, although we know that there is a good deal of discussion in other "perfect societies" about the aims and the justification of a penal code. We can only think of papal and episcopal authority in terms of monarchical structures, and we see other terms as a threat to that authority. We have ready answers to all questions within our system; outside it we are lost. It is our habit to rely on an undisputed tradition.

The Call for Teamwork

The difficulties involved in revising the Church's law are mainly due to the critical situation in which the study of canon law now finds itself. Our illustrious predecessors were fully acquainted with every aspect of their subject. They were exegetes, theologians, pastors and historians as well as canonists. As individuals, we are not, and if we are successfully to reconsider the whole of canon law in terms that will be understood in the twentieth century, we must do it together. This teamwork must, moreover, be done not simply by canonists, but by exegetes, theologians and others, together with canonists. What is so far lacking in the drafts of the new law of procedure and the new penal code is precisely a radical re-thinking of the significance of these laws in the light of Scripture, theology and the present life of the Church. It is not enough simply to reaffirm that these laws form an essential part of a perfect society. These elements of the Church's law were developed at a time when the Church had considerable authority in the secular sphere. Historians and sociologists would therefore seem to be indispensable members of a team responsible for revising canon law. The canonist's

contribution can only be his feeling for specifically legal relationships and his ability to systematize the relevant legal norms.

Consultation with the Bishops

As I said in my previous article in *Concilium*,[4] the Pope told
the Roman commission that the bishops would eventually be
asked to give their opinion about the schemes, as representatives
of the churches. It is clear, then, that they will first have to con-
sult everyone in their dioceses who can help them to judge the
results of the commission. The various schemes already available
will provide a reasonable basis for consultation, but no more than
this. This stage in the process of revision may well be more decisive than the present stage, but there must be enough time for
the teamwork to become operative. Either the members of the
Roman commission or the bishops might perhaps ask for this
teamwork to be done at the Catholic universities.

Interim Regulations

The revision of canon law is less urgent than the need for in-
terim provisions in the case of, for example, mixed marriages.
It was originally intended that the commission should be con-
sulted in connection with such regulations. Certainly it is desirable that the work of the commission and that of the various
bodies in the Roman Curia should be co-ordinated, but whether
this can be put into practice is another question. Where it is not,
very undesirable situations can arise. Let me give one example.

It has gradually become clear to all canonists, bishops' officials
and professors who have anything to do with matrimonial cases
that the Congregation for Faith has altered the practice of dis-
solving marriages "in favour of the faith of a third party". This
is the dissolution of the marriage of two non-Catholics, one of
whom at least is not baptized. Previously, such a marriage was
regularly dissolved if the marriage was irreparably broken and if
a Catholic afterwards wanted to marry one of the partners who
did not want to join the Catholic Church. This was done "in
favour of the faith of a third party", that is, of the Catholic.

For some months now, whenever a dissolution of this kind
has been sought, the answer has been *pro nunc non expedit*, "at

[4] *Op. cit.*, p. 132.

the moment undesirable". Quite by chance, I learnt that someone had heard from the prefect of the Congregation that the
theological arguments for the possibility of such a dissolution
were no longer very clear. No one has been officially informed
that the practice has been changed and no reasons have been
given. The bishops' officials were simply given a negative answer
to their requests. This means that hundreds, even thousands of
people had learnt, officially, from the Church that they had to
be patient but that they would be able to marry. They may therefore have made important and possibly irrevocable decisions.
Clearly, canon lawyers have the very important task of trying to
prevent such painfully unjust situations from occurring.

Translated by David Smith

Ingo Hermann

Conflicts and Conflict Resolution in the Church

FOR ABOUT twenty-five years work has been going on to develop a science of peace and conflict research,[1] but these attempts seem to have left no trace on the Catholic Church. In spite of the participation of individual Catholics and Catholic organizations (such as Pax Christi) in the work of this new science,[2] and in spite of the West German church's membership of the "German Association for the Promotion of Peace and Conflict Research", the findings of modern conflict analysis have not yet been applied to the Church. This is all the more surprising since the intensity and bitterness of conflict in the Roman Catholic Church have increased steadily since the convocation of the Second Vatican Council. What previously were interpreted as more or less fruitful "tensions", mere differences of approach, and were at least apparently resolved by verbal compromises or authoritative measures, now increasingly take on the character of open conflicts.

"Conflict" is used here in Johan Galtung's sense to describe the structure of a system within which there exist mutually irreconcilable concepts of the goal of the system, such that the achievement of one goal would exclude the achievement of the

---

[1] Cf. D. Senghaas (Ed.), *Friedensforschung und Gesellschaftskritik* (Munich, 1970), pp. 7–21; P. Noack, *Friedensforschung—ein Signal der Hoffnung?* (Freudenstadt, 1970); K. Kaiser, *Friedensforschung in der Bundesrepublik* (Göttingen, 1970).

[2] Cf. G. Scharffenorth/W. Huber (Eds.), *Bibliographie zur Friedensforschung, Studien zur Friedensforschung*, Vol. 6 (Stuttgart and Munich, 1971)

other.[3] In the case of conflicts within the Church and conflicts between Church and society it is now clear that norms and attitudes designed to resolve *tensions* (e.g., understanding the unity of the Church as uniformity, Rome's claim to authority, demands for obedience, the absorptive capacity of church organizations, religious humility) have proved quite unsuited to resolving *conflicts*. On the contrary, the methods in use so far, perfected over the centuries, for apparently dealing with conflicts only embitter and intensify existing and future conflicts. Apart from a number of material causes (which will be discussed later), the most important cause of this situation is an extremely simple and formal one: as long as a conflict (in Galtung's sense) is not recognized, acknowledged and treated as a conflict, but disguised, reinterpreted or smoothed over, there can only be apparent solutions which simply deal with symptoms. A proof of this hypothesis will be offered later.

First we must ask what attitude we can expect the Roman Catholic Church to have towards its own conflicts. Since all systems and societies at a pre-democratic stage of consciousness must have a disturbed attitude towards conflict, we may presume that the Church also will have a disturbed attitude towards conflict, in other words, that neither its structures nor its personnel will be capable of dealing adequately, that is, rationally and creatively, with its internal and external conflicts.

The structural inability to adopt a rational attitude towards conflict is the result of a paternalistic *leadership structure*, a *legal structure* biased in favour of the institution and authority, and a hierarchical *organizational structure*, co-ordinates in terms of which conflicts can only be seen as asymmetrical, i.e., as disputes

---

[3] Johan Galtung, "Theorien des Friedens", in *Krieg oder Frieden*, ed. J. Schlemmer (Munich, 1970), p. 135. This definition is used by Galtung primarily in connection with international conflicts, but can also be applied to social and psychological conflicts. In this article, the spheres of international, social and psychological conflict will not be kept strictly separate. In my opinion the application of conflict research to a church should not begin with distinctions based on conflict theory or rigid definitions, but with descriptions of problems tied closely to observation. Otherwise there is a risk of overlooking conflicts specific to churches. On theory and experience, cf. Th. W. Adorno and U. Jaerisch, "Anmerkungen zum sozialen Konflikt heute", in *Gesellschaft, Recht und Politik, W. Abendroth zum 60. Geburtstag* (Neuwied, Berlin, 1968), pp. 1-19.

between unequal partners.[4] The personal inadequacy for a rational attitude towards conflict results from the fact that neither the leadership élites nor the communities possess a theory which allows them to adopt an autonomous attitude to conflict, and so to create a symmetrical conflict situation with equal partners. The presumption of inadequacy in structures and personnel is supported by observation of the actual attitude within the Church to conflict and by a consideration of the absence of any element of conflict theory in theology and the sociology of the Church. This *blindness to conflict* in theory and practice gives us no grounds for a moral criticism of the Roman Catholic Church, however, at least in so far as the whole of present-day religious, philosophical, political and social thought, even in the social sciences, has been marked by a neglect of conflict which is no longer justifiable today.[5] According to Ralf Dahrendorf,[6] "for a considerable number of sociologists and the overwhelming majority of practitioners in economics, politics and other fields", there still exists today what he described in controversy with the American sociologists Elton Mayo and R. K. Merton as "a naïveté bordering on the incredible". This is the view that the normal condition of society is integration, the balanced functioning of the system in which each individual, group and institution has its own place and task in the structure of the world. Where conflicts exist, they can only be ascribed to individual pathology, that is to meta-social causes. Social conflicts are only the projections on to social relations of psychological disturbances (p. 116). From a functional point of view, they are a disturbance, and are for that reason dismissed as unimportant for political and moral theory (p. 117). "On this view conflict is a sociologically arbitrary phenomenon which disturbs the co-operative system of society.

[4] On the categories of symmetrical and asymmetrical conflict, cf. J. Galtung, "Theorien", p. 136.

[5] In West Germany this situation has been discussed particularly clearly by R. Dahrendorf, e.g., *Gesellschaft und Freiheit* (Munich, 1961), cf. esp. pp. 112–32, 197–235. For an informative introduction to the whole problem, see also L. A. Coser, *The Functions of Social Conflict* (London, 1956).

[6] Cf. note 4. This reference to Dahrendorf does not imply acceptance of his hypostasizing of conflict as a supra-historical engine of social change. Dahrendorf developed this view from the works of Georg Simmel. Cf. Th. W. Adorno and U. Jaerisch, "Konflikt heute", pp. 17 f.

This is the logic of utopia; it is the logic of the totalitarian treatment of deviants" (p. 117).

In order to measure the significance of the sociology of conflict for theology, we must now transpose the discussion from sociological into theological language. From the idea of the organism in Paul, and ancient thought generally (cf. Menencus Agrippa; 1 Cor. 12. 12–30), to the interpretation of the Church as a *"societas perfecta"*, the foundations were laid for a situation in which conflict in the Church could only be seen as a dysfunctional disturbance, a destructive threat to the whole system. Of itself, the Church's self-understanding offers little likelihood of understanding conflict as a normal element in the life of a humane religious community. The incorrect interpretation of "unity" as conformity and uniformity contributed to an oversimplified view of conflicts as schisms, and thereby also avoided the need for a serious discussion of the workings of the system. The history of dogmas and the history of the Church will certainly require far-reaching revision in the light of the sociology of conflict, and this demand cannot be dismissed by warnings against "reducing the Church to a sociological concept". Like history in general, church history is written by the winners, and in each case it is essential to the winners to portray the other side exclusively as a pathological element and a cause of the instability.

These remarks would be cynical if they were not based on an understanding of the social and theological function of conflict which regards conflict affecting religion and the Church also as a part of civilized life. A further reference to Dahrendorf will support this view and show its connection with the theological idea *"ecclesia semper reformanda"*: Dahrendorf sees the meaning and importance of conflict as the maintenance and promotion of change in social systems (*op. cit.*, p. 124). The general connection between conflict and change is obvious.

What, then, is the meaning of the polarity between government and opposition? One group would be enough simply to maintain the existing system, while if the opposition were only a pathological element, a cause of instability, it would be superfluous. The obvious significance of the interplay between government and opposition lies "in keeping the political process alive, in discovering new ways through argument and discussion and

thereby maintaining the creative quality of human societies"
(Dahrendorf, *op. cit.*, p. 126). It is not conflict and change which
are pathological deviations from the norm, but much more
rigidity and inability to change which are symptoms of the weakness of a system: "Only a totalitarian society in practice knows—
at least in appearance—that general agreement and unity, that
grey single sameness, which is the mark of the *societas perfecta*"
(Dahrendorf, *op. cit.*, p. 128).

If we apply these considerations from conflict theory to the
Roman Catholic Church, the first result is a complete rehabilita-
tion of conflict in the Church, for so long suspect both in theology
and in practice. Those who formulate or make conscious conflicts
in the Church can no longer be written off as quasi-criminal or
psychologically unstable rebels. Conflicts can no longer be seen
as dysfunctional disturbances, but must be understood as a normal part of the life of the Church. Analysis in terms of conflict
theory would certainly presuppose a radical change of consciousness in the Church, which it would itself also help to bring
about. Such a change in the theoretical framework can only be
expected, however, if a corresponding practice for dealing with
conflict is established. The Church can only learn to think properly about conflicts when it learns to live with conflicts. This
ability is too complex an interrelation of different forms of behaviour and different reactions to be described here. Nevertheless, since we are concerned with problems of practice, and since
practice can only be adequately conceived in specific historical,
social and political contexts, it may be legitimate methodologi-
cally to suggest some prerequisites which seem particularly important, in view of the present situation in the Church, for the
introduction of a possible method for dealing with conflicts.
There are three "discoveries" which the Roman Catholic Church
needs to make in the second half of the twentieth century: it
needs to discover communication, emancipation, and the Church
as a group.

I. THE DISCOVERY OF COMMUNICATION

The theory and practice of communication are among the
most important objects of conflict and peace research. It is

impossible to analyse and describe, let alone solve, international, domestic and social conflicts without an adequate understanding of the actual and possible channels of communication between the parties.[7] Karl Deutsch, in his *Politische Kybernetik*,[8] quotes Norbert Wiener, the father of cybernetics—which Deutsch describes as "the systematic scientific investigation of the processes of communication and control in organizations of all kinds".[9] Wiener stated in 1955: "Communication is the cement which holds organizations together. Only communication enables a group to think, see and act in common."[10]

In order not to give too great an ideological weight to the concept of communication in its application to the problems of dealing with conflict in the Church, it should be noted that the concept of communication is used at this point in a quite restricted sense, in its sociological and cybernetic dimension. "Communication" will be understood here as "the ability to transmit messages and respond to them".[11] Seen in these terms, communication is a problem of information, of the flow of information within a system and between a system and its surroundings. If we now wish to consider the discovery of communication as a first prerequisite for a rational attitude towards conflict within the Church, we shall have to analyse the Church's information structures. This is an empirical task which has not yet been carried out. A first glance at the problem produces merely observational data, which however can claim a measure of agreement among numerous observers with different standpoints.

First Datum. Leaving aside questions of its theological justifiability, the actual structure of the Roman Church is hierarchical and gives a similar structure to the flow of information in the Church. Information flows in one direction, from above to below, there is no feed-back, and the declining level of information finally leads to a shortage of reliable information "at the

---

[7] Cf. K. W. Deutsch, *Politische Kybernetik, Modelle und Perspektiven* (Freiburg, 1969); cf. also M. L. Cadwallader, "Die kybernetische Analyse des Wandels", in *Theorien des sozialen Wandels*, ed. W. Zapf (Cologne and Berlin, 1970), pp. 141–6.
[8] Cf. K. Deutsch, *Kybernetik*, p. 11.
[9] Cf. K. Deutsch, *Kybernetik*, p. 126.
[10] Cf. K. Deutsch, *Kybernetik*, p. 127.
[11] Cf. K. Deutsch, *Kybernetik*, p. 128

base", i.e., in the local community. The ordinary member of the Church experiences pronouncements, decisions and actions of the leadership only as *faits accomplis, ex cathedra*, as instructions, from the pulpit, or through the publication of previously censored (*imprimatur*) opinions. Communication as an exchange of opinions, completely open argument and decision, a two-way flow of information is at present neither possible nor desired In relation to the hierarchy, members of the Church are entitled to indoctrination but not information.

Second Datum. As well as the possibly theologically justifiable hierarchical structure, with the episcopacy at the centre, a para-hierarchical structure has become established in the course of time, centred on the central administration or curia in Rome. For curial organizations, even local hierarchies are no more than regional representatives. The flow of information (in this case not from above to below but from the centre to the periphery) transmits information not as information but as administrative instructions. Feed-back is not provided for, but can occasionally be forced out of the administration by protests (as in the case of the so-called *lex fundamentalis*). Feed-back set up in response to pressure frequently leads, however, to "expulsion trials" in important cases, e.g., Vatican I, in which the opposition is first forced into isolation and then labelled a schism.

Third Datum. The flow of information between the system and its surroundings does not correspond to the standard expected in open societies. If we ask whether and in what form the Church is present at any particular time in its host society, our answer today must be that the Church is present to the extent that it constitutes a political force. The mass media and the public only notice the Church in so far as it is politically relevant. The looser the connection between the Church and political power, the weaker is its cybernetic presence. Various conclusions can be drawn from this state of affairs. One implies an effort to make the Church a political force, which means turning it into an interest or pressure group, involving links with the prevailing political and economic forces and the corresponding adaptations, compromises and entanglements. Another conclusion from the contemporary interdependence of social presence and political power is the resolve to break the connection, which has nothing to do with the essence of religion or Christianity, and for the Church no longer to make claims to political power, but to make its presence felt through information. This line of argument brings us into the context of open and democratic societies, and also connects with the rediscovered understanding of what preaching once was and can be. This implies the need to examine the relation of the Roman Catholic Church to the information media. The inadequacy of this relation has been convincingly established, by K. W. Bühler[12] for the Protestant and by E. M. Lorey[13] for the Catholic Church.

II. The Discovery of Emancipation

Peace and conflict research has its own educational theory. Any educational theory today must be regarded as a contribution to the *emancipation* of man. The way to this goal is called *enlightenment*. This very compressed summary, which may sound like a collection of slogans and empty formulas, will be given meaning when I fill in the connection between social and international conflicts and their social origins, particularly those deriving from the sociology of groups. This makes it clear that any practice for coping with conflict—if we are not content to see it in functionalist terms as mere external direction—must depend to a great extent on enlightenment and a desire for emancipation in the groups involved. What do I mean in this context by "educational theory", "enlightenment" and "emancipation", and how do they help us to discover the preconditions for a rational attitude to conflict in the Church? If peace is to be more than harmonization and a smoothing over of differences, a total dedication of human intelligence will be required in all areas of society. For a religious group, this implies unconditional support for more education, more rationality and more enlightenment. Unfortunately, for two hundred years the Catholic—and to a large extent also the Protestant—leadership élite has tried to avoid the intellectual and political challenge of secular enlightenment. This opposition, and the dismissal of a phenomenon in Western intellectual history as "rationalism", is understandable,

[12] *Die Kirchen und die Massenmedien* (Hamburg, 1968).
[13] *Mechanismen religiöser Information* (Munich and Mainz, 1970).

since enlightenment is always total, and challenges taboos and claims to domination. But this opposition cannot be justified if we remember the impulses towards enlightenment and emancipation contained in the prophetic element of the Old and New Testaments, and if we realize that any concept of humanity must involve maturity—and it was Kant who defined enlightenment as "man's emergence from his culpable immaturity". There can be no resolution of conflict without rationality, no rationality without enlightenment, and no enlightenment which does not lead to the emancipation of man. This is why the Church must learn to release man from its tutelage and to permit and promote education for emancipation, even in theology.

III. The Discovery of the Church as a Group

Even today it is possible to meet an attitude—often in the interpretation of New Testament texts or the appropriation of New Testament concepts—which says *ekklesia* and means the Roman Catholic Church. In spite of this neglect of theological nuances, it has been evident at least since the Reformation, and recognized since Vatican II, that the plurality of Christian churches which has grown up in the course of history makes any absolute claim on the part of one church impossible. It has also been evident at least since the end of the Middle Ages, and impossible to ignore since the French Revolution, that the Church and society are not identical and that churches as institutions seen by sociology form parts of the wider society. These two facts make it clear that in sociological terms the Christian churches must be regarded as groups.[14] This truism would not have to be mentioned if the churches had drawn the appropriate conclusions from their character as groups for their external relations and above all for their internal structure. This is, however, not the case. As far as external relations are concerned, the Church slips into the role of a social group when this is to its advantage and when it has no other possibility of participating in social life. This is the case, for example, in the U.S.A. and West Germany. The role

[14] It is obvious that "group" does not necessarily mean "pressure group". On the concept of the group cf. R. König (Ed.), *Soziologie*, Fischer-Lexikon (n.e. 1967), pp. 112–19.

of a group is nevertheless alien to the Roman Catholic Church's official and traditional self-understanding. A glance at the relations between Church and State as set out in the code of canon law, or in concordats, leaves no doubt that in the eyes of the Vatican social relations such as those in Italy, Spain or Portugal are regarded as more suitable than those in secularized states.[15]

From the point of view of an approach to conflict, the group character of the Church is particularly important in its internal structure. In this case it is not self-understanding which constitutes the group; the Church is structurally a group, whether or not this is recognized and accepted. All the features which characterize a group can be found in the Christian churches: élite formation and leadership structure, authority pyramid, pecking order, Parkinson's Law,[16] Peter Principle,[17] in-group and out-group attitudes, the tendency to eliminate nonconformist or critical elements. All these are laws and behavioural models which are as applicable to the Church as to parties, bureaucracies, regimes and businesses. They are the structural laws of large and small groups, from which religious groups are not exempt. Only when this is realized will it be possible to analyse the conflict formations within the Church, to distinguish between the legitimate and illegitimate claims of hierarchy and laity, and even eventually to go beyond this dichotomy and replace new and existing patterns of friends and enemies by a genuine awareness of conflict. This development would mean the end of ill-considered group egoism at the expense of those outside and of group-centred models of behaviour within the group; it would make it possible to replace terror by tolerance[18] and to establish rational resolution of conflicts.

These conditions for a new attitude to conflict, which I have done no more than outline, imply not only a radical change of consciousness but corresponding structural reforms. Indeed, this

[15] Cf. J. Neumann, I. Hermann, *Braucht die Kirche ein Recht?* (Düsseldorf, 1970), p. 70.

[16] Cf. C. N. Parkinson, *Parkinson's Law* (Boston, 1957; London, 1958).

[17] Cf. L. J. Peter and R. Hall, *The Peter Principle* (London and New York, 1969).

[18] S. P. Hengsfeld, I. Hermann, *Die Alternative zum Terror. Pluralismus in Theologie und Kirche* (Düsseldorf, 1970).

connection between a change in consciousness and reform high-lights the limitations and possibilities in the Roman Catholic Church for a new theory and practice with regard to conflict, based on an equality of rights between all parties.

There are limits, because the demands made by the system as a whole on groups and individuals can only be defined from out-side (by the society), not from within, and yet the confrontations which are decisive from the point of view of conflict must take place in the area of these demands, over attitudes to minorities, critical intellectuals, nonconformists and opposition groups.[19] These situations take on a special importance in any analysis of the conflicts facing the traditional structure of the Church as a result of the revolutionary change in theological and sociological self-understanding which is at present taking place among the clergy, the system's leadership élite. In general, the only possi-bility for groups or individuals who are open to change, pro-gressive or nonconformist, is emigration, secession or at least disengagement, in sociological language, a dissociative attitude. The conflict is clearest in the case of the laicization of priests. This is an example of conflict in Galtung's sense (see above). The system and the individual are unequal partners, and the conflict is therefore asymmetrical. The weaker partner, the priest who has decided to be laicized, can preserve his identity only through dissociation. An associative attitude would only be possible if the conflict could be made symmetrical by fairness and self-restraint on the part of the system. There is, however, little likelihood of such a change at present. The official Roman Church's attitude is still based almost entirely on group-centred defence mechan-isms; anyone whose attitude does not tend to support the stability of the system and the *status quo* is dismissed as ill or amoral and neutralized by the use of pejorative labels.[20]

Nevertheless, there are some hopes for the twofold require-ment of a change of consciousness and structural reform. Changes

---

[19] Cf. I. Hermann, K. D. Ulke, *Die unerwünschten Aufklärer, Die In-tellektuellen und die Kirche* (Düsseldorf, 1970).

[20] Cf. Ingo Hermann, "Es geht nicht ohne Theorie, Römische Schwierig-keiten mit dem Zölibat", in *Die Christen und ihre Konflikte* (Olten, 1970), pp. 25-38; L. Waltermann (Ed.), *Rom, Platz des Heiligen Offiziums*, no. 11 (1971).

in a community which derives from Jesus of Nazareth can only take place through a return to that source. In other words, reform and advances in consciousness are only possible through a re-instatement of an evangelical attitude in the churches. If this took place, the power of Jesus' evangelical attitude would be released, and would lead, among other things, to humane atti-tudes to conflict. The New Testament understanding of dynamic freedom and plurality, of love and humanity, could provide a vigorous stimulus to the introduction of adequate attitudes to conflict.

Progress in this direction can be made only through the official adoption of techniques for dealing with conflict. Here, finally, I shall refer only to the two most important of these: open con-frontation and institutional guarantees for discussion. It is neces-sary to mention these mainly because any attempt to analyse conflict within the Church will face fierce opposition.[21] Not every-one will welcome the enlightenment, growth in autonomy and destruction of taboos which would be produced by an analysis of conflict. Those who have reason to fear publicity will attempt to prevent conflict research and its application to churches and religions.

The situations I have so briefly outlined in this article require further investigation. For this reason I make the following sug-gestion for practical political action. An international, inter-denominational, scientific institute for social conflict should be set up, to be independent of the administration and hierarchy of the Christian churches. It would be composed of conflict and peace researchers from various countries, religions and social systems. It would be financed by a foundation whose basic re-sources would be provided by the Christian churches, and work in collaboration with all existing centres for peace and conflict research. Its particular task would be to investigate the causes of social conflict and to set up a special department to apply the methods and results of conflict analysis to churches and religions.

[21] On the opposition to critical peace research, cf. D. Senghaas, *Friedens-forschung und Gesellschaftskritik*, p. 8.

Translated by Francis McDonagh

PART II
DOCUMENTATION

Some Examples of Reform in Local Churches

1. *Church Reform in Bohemia*

Jiří Němec/Bonaventura Boůse

I. INTRODUCTION

OBVIOUSLY problems of church reform cannot be considered exhaustively from only one viewpoint. The authors of the present article are nevertheless forced to restrict themselves to only one—the pastoral—aspect of the theme. They are quite aware that this viewpoint can allow only a reference to the basic complex of problems. The theme has to be defined negatively: we are concerned neither with sociological problems nor with questions of church law or politics. Since today it is impossible to conceive of pastoral affairs without the contributions of sociology of religion and other sciences, we shall presuppose various publications in these areas as the indirect background of this article.[1] In addition, we must add that it is part of the specific situation of the Church in which we live that it is to a great extent subject to historical inertia, that is: its present state is conditioned by an often very distant past. Therefore we cannot avoid some reference to Czech church history. If we want to understand the (to some extent appreciable) difficulties of the pastoral work of the Catholic Church in Bohemia, we must not only be aware of the historical roots of its organizational structures, but must recognize its mentality: its self-conception, its anxieties and its customs.

---

[1] Cf. E. Kadlecová, *Eine soziologische Untersuchung der Religiosität des nordmährischen Kreises* (Prague, 1967); J. Radouchova, "The Czechoslovak State and the Catholic Church after February 1948", in *Revue dejin socialismu*, Prague, Vol. 9, 1969, pp. 37-62.

II. HISTORICAL DEVELOPMENT

Since the end of the Middle Ages, Bohemia has been an area of reformist movements, which were theologically weak yet characterized by great moral sincerity and a striving for a living truth derived from the Bible. The oldest Czech translation of the Bible was made in the second half of the fourteenth century: the ordinary people's acquaintance with it was already a matter for astonishment to foreigners in the fifteenth century.

Czech Catholicism arose only after Trent as a reaction against Reformation trends—and one supported by the ruling court. After the victory of the House of Habsburg at the beginning of the seventeenth century, it was carried through with all available force—often despite the objections of the Jesuit and Capuchin missionaries entrusted with the "spiritual" aspect of the Counter-Reformation. This link with the State remained so strong, even in subsequent years, that from the middle of the eighteenth century the Czech church changed from a feudal triumphalist church into a bureaucratic one wholly dependent on the State. The church tried to withstand the onslaught of liberalism from the middle of the nineteenth century by forming societies and political parties—but without any profound understanding of the needs of the people, whose discontent with the social order and political suppression increased. For this reason, from the beginning of the nineteenth century, the tension increased between the rich and bureaucratized state church and the people; this tension was "romantically enlightened" in terms of memories of the Czech reformist movement of the past and finally culminated in the break-with-Rome movement of the laity and the lower clergy at the start of the nineteen-twenties.

Men of broad intellectual vision such as T. G. Masaryk, E. Rádl or J. L. Hromádka still put their hope at that time in Czech Catholicism; they drew some inspiration from the tradition of the Czech Reformation, although they were somewhat critical of its popular interpretations. The reaction of the Catholic intellectual circles to this situation was characteristic: they tried to resolve their inner contradictions by means of an exaggerated apocalypticism and Marian revelations, and a revived Romanticist adoration of the Middle Ages, together with the chiliastic visions of Léon Bloy; they attempted to conclude the disputes with the hierarchy in favour of the hierarchy by means of an excessive emphasis on the role of the papacy and Rome. Apart from a few attempts to reform the Catholic Church from within, these circles were characterized mainly by their lack of social awareness. In spite of the less propitious atmosphere within the Church after Vatican I, from the middle of the nineteenth century until the eve of the great break-with-Rome movement after World War I there were many different attempts at reform. These efforts were, however, broken up by that post-war impulse, or—in so far as people remained in the Church—neutralized. A series of ideas formulated after 1918 by the priests' organization, "The Union of Czechoslovak Pastors", which included about 90% of the Czech clergy, anticipated Vatican II (e.g., in the reform of the liturgy, the reformulation of regulations for studies for the priesthood and for education) and other modern provisions (permission for cremation). Some other questions of that time have remained open to this day: the Czechoslovak patriarchate, the self-administration of the church, voluntary celibacy.[2]

III. The Present Position

In our country, official Roman Catholic Christianity still tries to see itself as the strongest Christian denomination in the nation, which is still religious and lives on the basis of Christian, and especially Catholic tradition. This presupposition is not subjected to any critical examination. The administrative structure is artifically retained as it was introduced after Trent (Moravia still possesses the pre-Tridentine structure): a network of regional parishes, half of which are only formally still in existence. Great care is taken to preserve the old sacred buildings to which divine service is confined, for they are seen as symbols of and necessary to the existing structure. The priests who exercise their office in these churches are isolated by training and way of life from the faithful whom they should serve. Proclamation by means of the sermon, which occurs exclusively in traditional forms of divine

---

[2] "The renewal of the Catholic Church in the Czechoslovak Republic." A draft paper for the Union of Czech Pastors in Prague (Prague, 1919).

service, is of little account, since it is often addressed to fictive, unreal men and resolves non-existent problems. Despite external linguistic and ritual changes,[3] divine service has retained its sacral and (seen externally) its magical character. It does not pertain to the life of those who attend it, but on the contrary attempts to remove them from their everyday life and to introduce them to another, "sacralized" world. Those who enter a church only to watch the liturgy or at the best to take part in a "play" with the priest, are not a church, that is an assembly in the name of Christ. There is no relationship between them and no feeling of community. At the most, there is subjective uplift for the individual by means of singing and recitation; the priest is heard out patiently, and Holy Communion is received—which is the expression of private piety wholly separated from the Church. Theologically trained Christians will take this sort of divine service merely as a fulfilment of duty. Simple people will be kept in a formal and formalistic religiosity which is far removed from actuality. These sermons and services are nowadays the only living indication of the official Roman Catholic Church in Czechoslovakia.[4]

The foregoing shows that Catholicism as a whole does not appear as a church: that is, as a community bearing witness to Christ. There is none of those living communities, in which the church is realized and revealed; true dioceses and parishes are not formed. Pastoral councils and priests' councils have not taken on and there are no lay councils. The faithful whom in the end priests are supposed to serve have no voice in the appointment of priests. Nevertheless there is a growing desire among the laity for community in the church. To the extent that the prerequisites

---

[3] A new order for the Mass came into use in translation on 30 November 1969; it was not, however, gradually introduced beforehand. In most churches the old uses, cancelled by the new order, nevertheless survive. The possibilities made available by the compromise order have not been taken advantage of. The formal (superficial) introduction of the new order of the Mass has led to a delay in any real overall development. The new marriage services were introduced only at Easter 1970 but the new service for infant baptisms has still not been published, even though it is a year since the translation was approved. The translation of the burial service was completed last Autumn, but has not yet been approved.

[4] Cf. B. Bouše, "The Hopes of Catholicism in Bohemia", in *Duchovní pastýř* (Prague), Vol. 20, January 1971, pp. 11–13.

for this are present, i.e., if they can find a priest who is ready to answer their needs, they form spontaneous nuclear communities and the decayed parishes begin to come to life again. It is obvious that in these emergent communities the Church is to a large extent not yet fully realized. Pietistic subjectivism and inadequate awareness of societal (and especially of social) requirements survive in them, and their initial development is still endangered by the chance nature of the conditions governing their existence.

IV. Ecumenical Tasks

From what has been said about the historical presuppositions of the present situation of Catholicism in Czechoslovakia, some idea is possible of the tasks for ecumenism in all its aspects. Naturally we understand ecumenism as one dealing with essentials, that is, an ecumenism of the diverse ecclesiastical denominations in their striving to realize the Christian mission—in other words this does not mean ecumenism as any kind of ritual exchange between the leading functionaries. On this point it should be noted that ecumenism in Czechoslovakia in the last few years has become adequately acclimatized, and that common services of the word, bible hours and lectures with subsequent discussion have become the rule in various places. Recently, however, the official meetings of the leading representatives of the churches have been discontinued. One of the reasons for this is the attitude of the Czech bishops and ordinaries to the papal *motu proprio* on mixed marriages. In fact, in its interpretation of this already intrinsically problematical *motu proprio*, the Czech episcopate has so far retreated in the direction of the original anti-ecumenical standpoint, that this became an inducement to the non-Catholic churches to cool down contacts. This process has not been without effect on the life of the churches.

V. Tensions in the Church

It is important to realize the connections between the church structure to date in Czechoslovakia, a certain mentality in the Church, and a certain theology (ideology) which systematizes and justifies these phenomena. That the priest relies on the actuality of what is known to scholastic theology as *opus operatum*, is often the reason why the priest is chiefly concerned with the externals of the liturgy and not at all with a personal relation to the liturgy and what it does or should express; nor does he feel the need for any personal relationship with the "spectators", if he is to fulfil his "function". Consciously or unconsciously, he lives by the conviction that the liturgical activities he carries out and the text he recites do not lose their value even when they are carried out and recited carelessly, or thoughtlessly. An actual sin or offence to God can nevertheless be of value if externals are nicely observed, since an imaginary "church" guarantees their inwardly inauthentic action. This priestly attitude, which is often imitated by the faithful in their practice of their religion, is principally responsible for the magical character of the liturgy.

Similarly, some manifestations of the episcopate are fetishized in the church. This is a question not only of such occasions as confirmations and pilgrimages, but above all of the extraordinarily widespread conviction that the bishops are possessed of some special supernatural ability which enables them to solve a whole range of theoretical and practical or organizational questions, thus replacing a normal expert training and judgment. On the side of organization this idea corresponds to a total underestimation of the local churches in favour of the episcopate, and the practical non-existence of any living mutual communication between the faithful, their bishops and priests and, of course, between groups.

It is obvious that tensions arise in every social structure. However the inadequate forms of organization and the paternalistic mentality of the Czech church do not make it possible to profit from these tensions; hence the result can be a neurotic, pathological atmosphere in the case of every new idea. One section of church members has retained the tendencies of the intellectual circles which existed in the Czech areas mainly in the period between the world wars. Their fear of the future sometimes leads them even to reject Vatican II. However, the resulting diaspora communities find great difficulty in obtaining any response to their justified demands, and are often suspected by the official representatives and the lower clergy of inadequate orthodoxy and lack of respect for authority. The bearers of authority wish, under the banner of a "defence" of Catholicism, to impose a uniformity which suppresses initiatives. But in this way the very thing that was to be defended is endangered: the catholicity of the Bohemian church. Its participation in the life of the world Church is jeopardized. The Bohemian church has taken up a position in which it cannot share unity of belief with the other Catholic churches, because its official representatives bring it virtually to the state of renouncing their struggles and tensions and judging their doubts and anxieties, modes of thought and striving for truth. In so doing it refers to the "heritage of the Fathers", to its often very dark and doubtful past. The popular Catholic press will even slander foreign churches. The Dutch church especially is presented by some ordinaries as a shocking example: there is even talk of the danger of "Hollandism".

In the background of this authoritarian mode of thinking there is that objectivistic, extrinsicist theology with which theology students are indoctrinated, using simplified extracts from neo-Thomist textbooks of the last years of the nineteenth century. Hence there is a certain social structure and a corresponding spiritual equivalent and guarantee. It would be illusive to imagine that in the matter of church reform in Czechoslovakia it would be possible to pass over this connection and artificially to separate the complex of problems involved. The main question remains: How is it possible to undertake church reform in such a situation, where is one to begin, and where must the main effort be concentrated?

VI. Prospects for the Future

Urbanization and industrialization, the growth of education and increased mobility of the population, conditioned—as much in Czechoslovakia as in other countries—a liberation of the individual from the traditional societal and psychological bonds and put the emphasis on the personal choice of a mode of life and church membership. Consequently the need became clear for a restructuring of pastoral work, announced in our church in the formation of typical diaspora communities; that is, functional or (as we call them) "personal" ministries. It is clear at the moment that there must be a *pluralism* of the entire pastoral structure. In other words, the spontaneous activity which comes from "below" must be supported: the hitherto obligatory model of a territorial ministry must be transcended, since it was in practice usefully reduced only to liturgical assemblies and occasional sacramental functions. The beginning of reform is therefore the formation of spontaneous groups, which try to find their liturgical expression and their place in the structure of social-charitable activity (here it is a question mainly of help for lonely and abandoned people, who have become isolated in contemporary industrial society): groups which ultimately are also looking for a theological consciousness which finds expression mainly in catechetical and cultural activity. The actual needs and the spirituality of these communities are already beginning to obtain an appropriate response from priests and theology students. The situation of these inspired people is still difficult at times, and on the other hand the existing form of preparation for the priesthood and the way of life of our priests inhibit the appropriate response. It is hardly probable that there will be any improvement so long as married men are not admitted to ordination, and above all so long as there is no change in the existing practice of celibacy in the Western Church, and women are not ordained. Perhaps this process will be speeded up by the lack of priests. In his work on "the present situation of priests in Bohemia", Z. Boháč writes:[5] "Only in order to fill some two-thirds of the official parishes in Bohemia (reckoning on an average thirty-five year ministry) the Bohemian seminary would have to put out forty students a year". This seminary produced forty-three this year, but—as has been the rule in recent years—many of them were already middle-aged. Therefore the estimate of their active life must be radically reduced.

Of great help to us would be some organizational and legal changes affecting the Church as a whole: a legal codification of the jurisdiction and effective power of the pastoral and lay councils within the structure of the Church, in which the emphasis would be on their co-responsibility for pastoral activity. In addition there should be a recognition of the legal status of parishes and dioceses, and a legal grounding of the inseparability of the

[5] In *Via* (Prague), Vol. 1, 1968, pp. 27-8.

social and charitable work of the Church and its liturgical activity. It should become an obvious rule that priests do not treat other Christians as an undifferentiated anonymous mass, which happens to have come together in the church and which breaks up again afterwards, but as a community in which there is always as a matter of principle a brotherhood, collegiality and dialogue of all Christians, in conciliarity and with representation allowing direct, equal and secret voting. This means that in every community there should be a bishop, priest or deacon who should have certain directive functions within certain limits, but that the community should also have its chosen representatives who also have their clearly defined area of responsibility in church law. Prejudices in this regard have mounted up in Bohemian Catholicism.

A reason for this is that the above-mentioned tendencies and requirements are very close to the old (and already long since condemned) reform and reformation movements in Czechoslovakia, which in this way would eventually be justified. Clearly, Bohemian Catholicism cannot avoid the as yet hardly apparent process of painful self-reflection which will probably run parallel to a formation of living Christian communities.

Translated by Verdant Green

2. *The Ecumenical Student Parish in the Free University of West Berlin*

Manfred Kramer/Thomas Gawron

THEOLOGIANS of various specialisms, particularly exegetes, have shown that the development of democratic principles of communication, organization and decision is not contrary to the structural principles of the Church, but is a consequence of a Gospel of freedom. They have also made clear that the Church is not a system of salvation isolated from society. As a community of those who try to live by the promises of God announced and finally confirmed in Jesus, the Church is always entrusted with the humanization of the social co-world.[1]

An increasingly large number of Catholics wish to draw practical conclusions from these insights—consequences for the structures of the Church and for parish life. The following report is intended to show (in terms of the Catholic university parish at the Free University of West Berlin) what are the problems and conflicts which can arise in the attempt to build a democratic and political community.

I. Student Parish and Reform

At the beginning of the student protest movement, a discussion of post-conciliar and above all of "political" theology took place among Christian students. The criticism by the radical-democratic and socialist groups of non-democratic and authoritarian structures in State and society, of the equanimity of many citizens in regard to the poverty and exploitation in industrial states and the "Third World" and the criticism of the tutelage exercised over society by means of diverse manipulative mechanisms in favour of the ruling class was also prepared by Catholic students. This criticism they applied to that of the authoritarian hierarchical structures and socio-political function of the Catholic Church. The active students of the Catholic student parish (KSG) were soon united in their analysis of the ossified and hence unchristian structure of the Church; the conclusions they drew were nevertheless contested during the "reformation" phase of the parish in the period 1967–8.

Some understood this structure as an organizational consequence of a faith which was in principle an ideology, and at that time rejected (like *Kritische Katholizismus*[2]) any kind of differentiation of faith, religion and church as a new attempt to immunize Christian belief from radical criticism. This criticism,

---

[1] Cf. J. B. Metz, *Theology of the World* (London, 1968).
[2] Van Onna, Stankowski, *Kritischer Katholizismus* (Frankfurt, 1969); M. Krämer, "Kritische und 'kritische' Katholiken", *Frankfurter Hefte*, Vol. 24, 10, pp. 697–704.

however, did not mean a total rejection of the institutional Church. It was conceived rather as a locus of agitation for subversive Socialist groups. The student parish was intended to serve in this process as a means of "entry" into Catholicism.

On the other hand, representatives of an orientation to "political" theology stressed the fact that the theoretical approach of *Kritische Katholizismus* prevented an analysis of multifarious and opposing religious, ecclesiastical and theological tendencies. In addition, as a result of a too global approach, it was impossible to acknowledge the increasing conflict between the church establishment and the critical Christians. The actual task was seen much more as one of examining the emancipatory contents of the Christian message and their handing down in history, and the practical consequences for confrontation with the ruling political forces and the established Church as a whole.

II. Student Parish in Conflict with the Official Church

After several meetings on the subject of the structure and self-understanding of the student parish, the second conception prevailed, as formulated in the introduction to the Summer 1969 programme: "This university parish conceives itself as the community of those who try to live their life after the model of Jesus in the actual requirements of our university and society . . . as unconditionally determined upon justice, freedom and peace. The inclusive key-word 'peace'—*shalom!*—means in Judaeo-Christian tradition neither a sentimental cancellation of all social conflicts and contradictions nor a cheap model of harmony, nor a static state of peace; instead *shalom* is the slogan for a movement of liberation. In it men are freed and encouraged for appropriate commerce with the possibilities of life which they ensure but which they have still to perceive themselves. Hence peace becomes a challenge to existing conditions, which have to be transcended for the sake of future possibilities."

In July 1968, after discussions over a year, the new constitution of the Catholic university parish (KHG) was agreed upon. The executive committee of the parish, elected from the representatives of various reform groups, and legitimated by the parish assembly, was commissioned to engage in discussions with the

Bishop of Berlin, Cardinal Bengsch, on the recognition of the new democratic constitution of the student parish and of the candidate for the office of student chaplain, Chaplain Wiesendanger, chosen by the parish assembly. These discussions were contested in the parish, not least of all because of the negative experiences of other progressive West Berlin groups, such as the "Democratic-Catholic Working Party". Without going into the unfortunate process in greater detail,[3] suffice it to say that after one ninety-minute discussion between Bishop Bengsch and the parish committee, the Bishop rejected the KHG as the successor of the KSG. He also refused to acknowledge the parish's candidate as the student chaplain. Instead, he was sent to a parish far distant from the university, and was later required on several occasions to cease his continuing contribution to the work of the KHG. Nevertheless, the parish rejected the Bishop's demand that it should drop the use of the term "parish", and stated that it would refuse this request as long as the Bishop gave no theological justification for his rejection.

The dialogue which the KHG attempted failed above all for the following reasons:

1. The KHG, which wanted to put a "political" theology into practice, was faced with an official Church which saw criticism of the hierarchical Church not as an activation of faith but as a flight from "belief" into mere criticism for its own sake. In this way the main conflict centred upon the relation of ecclesiastical ministry to the parish. Whereas the KHG interpreted the ecclesiastical ministry as a function of service from and for the parish, the representatives of the ecclesiastical hierarchy asserted that there was an unalterable distinction between the common priesthood of all believers and the special priesthood of the office of the Church.

2. The Berlin official church, on account of its social isolation from critical intellectuals, especially of the student generation, was not informed of their awareness of problems and their questions. Therefore it projected its experiences with anti-ecclesiastical propaganda during the Third Reich, but also in the German Democratic Republic in the nineteen-fifties and sixties (i.e., dur

---

[3] KHG, *Initiative*, Vol. 9, 3, pp. 17–20.

ing the "Cold War") on to the Catholic students' criticism of the ecclesiastical system.

It was not in a position to distinguish the Christian criticism of the institution from the anti-clerical criticism of Fascism, or even that of Stalinist Marxism-Leninism.

3. The historically grounded fear of criticism of the system proper was reinforced in Berlin by existing political conditions. The vulgar Marxist propaganda of the GDR against the Catholic Church drove the West-Berlin section of the Church (connected with the GDR bishopric) into political co-operation with anti-Communist conservatives. Against this background, propaganda (particularly that of the Springer Press) against the anti-authoritarian student movement was able to find an especially strong echo in Catholicism.

III. POLITICAL PARISH

The fruitless discussions of the KHG with the West-Berlin official church and the Bishop of Berlin, and the increasing conflicts at the Free University caused the parish in the Winter of 1968–9 to concentrate more strongly on university political confrontations. Together with the Evangelical student parish (ESG), which (already since 1963) had been involved in attempts at democratization in the university, the KHG supported the struggle of the radical-democratic and Socialist groups in the university against all attempts of the Berlin government to reform the traditional "cultural university" in the direction of a "technocratic university" without taking into consideration the political dimension of scientific and scholarly work as a genuine component of student education.

When, at the end of the first phase of student protest, i.e. the anti-authoritarian stage, which was oriented to the "critical theory of the Frankfurt school of sociology, the conflicts in the university came to a head, the student parishes entered the political arena together. They supported the protest strike against rustication processes introduced against certain activists in the movement. In a critical article in the student journal *FU-Spiegel*, however, the parishes opposed the activism of certain student groups: "In contradistinction to a dogmatic position which would necessarily lead the Socialist groups into isolation, the student parishes formulate as a perspective for discussion a strategy for united work among progressive lecturers, students and professors. This means a stop to heresy-hunting and calumniation of those who are still learning.... We ... request confrontation with the actual political opponents ... the technocrats ... of big industry, and so on."[4]

IV. Approaches to an Ecumenical Parish

Although the active parish members were no longer in a position to give common practical endeavours an ecumenical and theological basis, we cannot really speak of the conversion of the student parishes into a "political union" featuring no theological reflection, meditation or divine service in addition to its political commitment.[5] On the contrary, the parishes attempted, in various forms of divine service, and in seminars with representatives of "political" theology, and a meditation week in Taizé, to develop the relationship of faith, parish and political action. In these discussions, the question of confessional theology was soon relativized. For it became apparent that the common attempt to realize *shalom* made the question of confessional membership pointless. On the basis of common political work and theological reflection, the organizational boundaries of the two parishes were cancelled: responsibility for decisions was henceforth entrusted to the one parish assembly of the ecumenical student parish or community in the Free University. Henceforth there was only one administrative team for the ecumenical parish consisting of the ESG and the KHG.

V. Student Parish in Crisis

If the phase of university political commitment of the ESG and the KHG in 1969 had shown that a university parish could engage in politics within the university without surrendering its identity as a parish, 1970 showed that the fear that by its

[4] Cf. K. B. Hasselmann, *Politische Gemeinde* (Hamburg, 1969).
[5] H. Maier, *Kritik der politischen Theologie* (Einsiedeln, 1970), pp. 88 ff.

political activity a parish could be "subverted" by a single university faction was not true.

So long as the ESG, and later both student parishes, were recognized as a radical democratic group in the university, no other university group, whether Socialist (SDS) or Communist, showed any interest in subverting the parish. Since the end of the first phase of the student movement, the process of student enlightenment had nevertheless led to the formation of "Red cells". At the same time the attempts of the State authorities to put through a "technocratic university reform" in the university had increased. There was also a reinforcement of administrative pressure on the Socialist and Communist student organizations. For these reasons, representatives of one Red cell began to play with the idea of subverting the ecumenical parish for their own purposes, and thus escaping victimization by the authorities. These attempts occurred when the parish was choosing a nev chaplain in 1970–1.[6] Despite all their solidarity and active participation in the struggle against class structures and social immaturity, the members of the parish insisted that theological criteria could not be fixed in predetermined guidelines for political action, but could arise only from the actual parish's self-consideration as a parish, out of confrontation with and reflection on biblical witness in the actual situation. So far as members of the Communist Red cell have participated in the ecumenical parish since then, it has been in a situation in which the uniqueness of both groups is ensured within a relatively binding political orientation and on a concrete situational basis.

VI. Future of the Political Parish

The cessation of dialogue with the official church in West Berlin should not cause other university parishes or communities to close discussions with the institutional church and other student parishes. Each parish must examine its own possibilities for intensive communication, discussion and action.

[6] The ESG chaplain, Hasselmann, left the parish in Spring 1970; Chaplain Wiesendanger died in Summer 1970. The Evangelical and Catholic students of the ecumenical parish chose G. Altendorf (from Hamburg) as their joint new chaplain.

Of course, in the Federal Republic, on account of an increasingly intransigent institutional Church, increasing alienation, abandonment of or struggle against the institution by Christians are conceivable.[7]

Despite all distance from, or critical solidarity with, the Church, it is more obvious now than before that the members of student parishes are more aware of and more firmly reject their formation by an authoritarian Catholicism. Catholic education for the most part allows of only a one-track route in the socialization process, one which makes men incapable of recognizing alternatives, choosing between them and making decisions. Without the examination and overcoming of this Catholic past, it will be impossible for political parishes to develop and realize in an exemplary manner alternative models for a domination-free church.

Even though, as far as the political parish in Berlin in the last few years was concerned, action and enlightenment were primary tasks, after the conclusion of this phase of the student movement it has to undertake the analysis of an ossified neo-capitalist society. To the extent that it conceives of itself as part of a Socialist emancipation movement, it will be concerned to minimalize domination and to criticize within a pluralism of the Left any attempt of Communist groups to rigidify matters. The development of alternatives, and the detection of new or neglected problems in this pluralism, or the Socialist movement, must not lead to a distancing from emancipatory essentials.

"Political student parish"—this concept demands actual practical engagement in the future. The experiences of the ecumenical parish in Berlin are only a beginning.

Translated by Verdant Green

---

[7] Cf. the conflicts between the German bishops' conference and the German Catholic Students' Union: F. J. Trist, "Studenten zwischen Kirche und Politik", *Publik*, 8, 1971; E. Schmied, "Politisches Engagement oder geistiges Ghetto", *Publik*, 31, 1971.

3. Reform of the Church in the Archdiocese of Chicago

William McCready

THE development of the Church in Chicago has consisted of periods of intense activity punctuated by periods of hesitation and uncertainty. The ongoing reform of the Church exists within this framework. For purposes of this exposition, history will be divided into three eras: the pre-conciliar Church; the Church during the Council; and the post-conciliar Church. There are unique examples of reform in each era, and there are lessons for the current situation to be learned from the past.

The dominant characteristic of the pre-conciliar Church in this city was its concern for social action, and the dominant figure was the rector of the seminary, Mgr Reynold Hillenbrand. During the early nineteen-thirties there were many forces for change within the Chicago context. The diocesan newspaper, *The New World*, took a consistently liberal position on social issues, especially those concerned with work and the workers. Father Carrabine of the Society of Jesus touched the minds and consciences of many young people through Chicago Inter-Student Catholic Action (CISCA). Men and women such as James O'Gara, John Cogley, Ed Marciniak, Dorothy Day, Mr and Mrs Patrick Crowley, and many others, were each working to enable their Church to speak through them to their world. Into this fertile context came the thirty-three-year-old rector of the major seminary, Mgr Hillenbrand. It is still difficult to tell exactly what role he played during this era, but it was something of a combination between that of a charismatic leader and a filtering gatekeeper allocating resources to that part of the system best able to use them. To some he was a dominant personality for growth and liberal social change, whereas to others he was an autocratic manager who determined who would be allowed to do what. Whether by inspiration or machination or a typically

Chicago combination of both, Hillenbrand and those around him gave the diocese a decade of competent, capable Church penetration into the modern world. The Catholic social action programmes proliferated rapidly. The Catholic Labour Alliance and the Catholic Interracial Council, formed under the influence of Father Daniel Cantwell, tackled some of the burning social issues of the day. Small groups of students, businessmen, and their wives began meeting at schools and in parishes to discuss and execute those actions that their Christian beliefs guided them towards. The Cana Conference under Father John Egan held seminars and offered lectures to married couples that exposed them to some of the brightest lights of the American and European churches. It was a time of most productive activity. Five main reasons for this success were:

1. The hierarchical leadership provided the atmosphere where one could try and fail and try again.
2. The clerical liberals were very good at creating bases of popular support.
3. The clergy and laity showed the decision-makers that they could be useful to them.
4. Hillenbrand was a charismatic leader who gathered innovative people around him.
5. The laity were of relatively high status, which gave the programmes an aura of respectability.

As the time for the Second Vatican Council approached, everyone waited to see how their Church was going to move. Many experiments in social action and liturgical renewal had been started within the diocese and people were waiting to see if they were going to be approved or changed. They waited for a ruling on the question of birth control and proposed reforms of the marriage laws. They waited for the theologians and the hierarchy to tell them what it was going to be like to be Catholic in the future.

During the Council, enthusiasm ran high, and so did expectations. The Church was in the news regularly. Special features on major communications media extolled the process of change in an institution that changed very slowly and cautiously. Liberals waited to see if their programmes would bear fruit.

Liturgists waited to hear news about English Masses and more meaningful rites. Meanwhile in Chicago the leadership was not passing from the hands of the old to the young. New people were not moving into the organizations at a rate sufficient for replacement. The new forces of personalism and the failure of social action to cure all the problems to which it addressed itself had the effect of turning many of the young away from the course of public action.

After the Council there was a resurgence of activity and attempts were made to reinstate the programme approach that had been operating in an earlier era. The ecumenical thrust of the Council gave rise to the National Conference on Religion and Race in 1963. Significant progress was made in the area of ministry to the Spanish-speaking people in the diocese. The Cana Conference expanded its activities into the areas of clerical education and religious publications. The Chicago Area Lay Movement (CALM) provided tutors for several thousand inner city children. The Association of Chicago Priests (ACP) was created and continues to have an impact on the diocese. The Confraternity of Christian Doctrine programme, liturgy renewal programmes, Fathers Weber and Killgallen's work in religious education, all of these and more are extensions of the early liberal movements that have penetrated into the post-conciliar era.

However, the programmatic style of the early reformers was no longer so successful. The crowds weren't what they used to be. Vatican II emphasized the concept of what it meant to be a Christian as never before. It exposed a theological basis that most of the programmers had not been aware of. The new directions that had been sought for so long had come and they were not what people had expected. The post-conciliar theology stressed the new man, individual conscience, and the *metanoia*. It encouraged people to change from what they had been to what they could be. There was no way to programme this; there was no lecture series that could produce this effect. No courses could be given nor film strips shown that could change a human being from one who was cautiously testing out his world-view, to a believing Christian who could preach the Gospel to his world. This was a slower process of growing; of becoming a different person in a significant way.

Present attempts at reform in Chicago include the following five phenomena: small worship-groups; the ACP; religious education; social-action movements; and clerical political involvement. The small worship-groups include pentecostals, liturgy groups of all kinds, various discussion groups, and an assortment of "transparochial" parishes. All these are generally held together by a personalistic thrust that attempts to make religion evident in the lives of its members. They respond to a real need since the traditional modes of worship no longer satisfy the desire for intimacy expressed in modern personalism. The question, however, is whether they will be able to speak to the world they live in, or whether they will turn in upon themselves. In order to reach out they must learn to organize, and they must know what they want to say to the contemporary condition. Whether they will develop their ability to speak to the needs of modern men remains to be seen.

The ACP, on the other hand, has made its organizational skills felt from its very inception. The corps leaders of this organization were men trained under Hillenbrand and in the liberal social action tradition of getting things done. The ACP was a response to the need for a democratic voice within the Church and as such it has met with a fair amount of success. Its work in the area of personnel management has been particularly innovative. However, it has tended too frequently to focus on potential conflicts with the hierarchy; it now seems doubtful whether it will be a force for leadership, or a democratic forum for the settling of internal clerical problems. Topics such as the theological base of a priesthood, the relationship between priest and people, and the prophetic role of the priest have been dying from lack of exposure because of the attention given to the questions of obedience and celibacy. The ACP has suffered a steady erosion of membership from an early high of 1000 to a present 450. Whether this situation will change is still in doubt.

Many experiments are going on in religious education. They range from a few innovative CCD programmes to planned TV broadcasts over diocesan-owned facilities. Trained personnel have been hired by parishes to devise new programmes. The clients range from elementary school children to adults seeking to know more about their Church. The primary need here is for source materials. Those working in the area now are doing a fine job with what they have but additional resources will be needed very soon. A more pressing problem is the matter of co-operation among the agencies of education, primarily the schools. There is no central agency with real power, so each school operates on its own to a considerable degree. Co-operation is essential, and indications so far lead one to believe that the future of religious education here could go either way.

The social action movements begun in the pre-conciliar era are presently adjusting themselves to contemporary questions. The Cana Conference, CFM, the Young Christian Workers (YCW) and Students (YCS), are developing new leadership cadres and new bases of volunteer support. They may succeed and they may not. Some, like the Cana Conference, have moved into the area of supplying resources to other organizations through seminars and publications. It is more and more difficult for these groups to recruit large quantities of high quality people. If they continue to find and fulfil specific needs they will survive. Most have not as yet discovered what those needs are, or how they might fulfil them.

Perhaps the most controversial element of current reform is the increasing participation of priests in various socio-political organizations. Among other examples we have a priest-alderman on the city council, a priest co-chairman of a citizens' group battling city hall over tax reforms, and a priest-director of the local chapter of the American Civil Liberties Union. There is also significant involvement of priests in various community organizations seeking to create power bases for the redesigning of the allocation of resources within the city. Many of these organizations, such as the organization for a Better Austin (OBA), are modelled after the patterns established by Saul Alinsky, which automatically makes them controversial. These priests are concerned not so much with Church reform as with radical changes in the way power is utilized in society. However, their involvement raises questions of reform for the Church itself. A common difficulty in this case is that these men are delicately balanced between the secular and the religious dimensions of society. What happens to their foundation in the sacred when priests begin dealing with the more secular forms of symbolism such as demonstrations and legal battles is as yet an unanswered question. Some say this will reform the sacred symbols; others fear they will be destroyed; arguments can be made for both cases. To a great extent it depends on the wisdom of the priest himself, and for the present the issue is still in doubt.

In summary there are three areas of unsolved problems that make the future of Church reform in this diocese a doubtful concern:

1. Can the theological insights be operationalized and applied to concrete issues?
2. Can the authority relationships and the decision-making structure of the diocese be democratized?
3. Can the innovators acquire the ability to speak to the world around them rather than to those who already agree with their positions?

If satisfactory solutions can be found to these difficulties, the diocese will become a paradigm for local reform. If solutions can not be found, even those progressive steps begun in the past will slowly grind to a halt. The real question facing the contemporary priesthood and laity is whether they will be able to speak the Gospel as vigorously to their world as the liberals of the pre-conciliar Church spoke it to theirs. Only time will tell.

4. *Examples of Attempts at Reform in the Church of Ceylon*

Tissa Balasuriya

The Catholic Church in Ceylon before 1960

FOUR major world religions are represented in Ceylon: Buddhists 65%, Hindus 20%, Christians 9%, Muslims 6%; Roman Catholics form 7·5% of the total population. Marxism, too, has had a considerable impact on the people because of the work of the left-wing political parties during the past thirty-five years.

After one hundred and fifty years of persecution under the Dutch from 1650–1796, the Church in Ceylon grew in numbers (because of a population increase) and in terms of parishes, dioceses, schools and social services. The 800,000 Catholics, as a group, had better educational opportunities than the members of other religions. They were thus a more privileged group in society. The Catholic leadership was English-educated, Western-oriented, middle class and rather conservative socially, though a small group of intellectuals had agitated in the nineteen-forties for social changes of a reformist nature.

In the nineteen-fifties, the church in Ceylon shared with the universal Church a strongly "anti-Communist" attitude, which made the church socially defensive and conservative. It was like-wise on the defensive vis-à-vis the nationalist and pro-Buddhist trends since 1931; most had become especially marked since Independence in 1948. The church was then rather monarchical in its government, monolithic in its façade, middle class in its options, pietistic in its spirituality, and defensive and organiza-tion-minded in its pastorate. It is from this background that we have to understand the evolution of the church in the past ten years.

Socio-political changes . . . 1956 to 1961

In 1956 the voters replaced the hitherto powerful westernized right-wing government by a more socialist one led by Mr Banda-ranaike and including Marxists in the Cabinet. The first reaction of the church leadership was indifference to Sinhala Buddhist cultural policies, and opposition to socialistic measures. The climax of this Catholic attitude was reached when, in 1960, soon after its landslide election victory, the subsequent government of Mrs Sirimavo Bandaranaike set out to take over the private schools and training colleges. The Catholic opposition took the final form of a non-violent physical occupation of Catholic schools, rather than allow the government to nationalize them. However, after six weeks of such resistance, the Catholics had to submit unconditionally to the new law.

This defeat was the greatest shock that the Ceylon Catholic community received in one hundred and fifty years; it felt that its main effort of a century was not only brought to nought, but even rendered a potential danger to the faith of Catholic children. The Catholics were disappointed that their past pupils from other religions did not rally round to defend their schools in their hour of need. The manner in which the Catholic leadership capitulated without consulting the rank and file of the Catholic combatants, deeply undermined their confidence in the leadership of the bishops.

The church realized that it was a minority that could no longer fight the mainstream of national movements. The bishops for their part saw that they could never again mobilize the Catholics for a mass struggle. In February 1961, the Catholics were a defeated, divided, discouraged, disgruntled group without any sense of direction and mission.

Catholic Rethinking 1961–1965

For several months the Catholics suffered a collective gloom due to their defeat and inability to find alternative approaches to their mission. The bitterest blow was perhaps the support given by quite a few Catholics, including teachers, to the policy of the government in taking over the schools. The rethinking was helped by the government itself not proving to be so motivated by Marxism as it was made out to be in the heat of the controversy.

The impact of Pope John and of the Vatican Council began gradually to be felt through the preparatory literature and discussions. These opened the way to a possible rethinking and critique within the Church itself. The catechetical movement, which was given considerable impetus by Father Hoffinger's visit, was the first direction in which the rethinking took shape. This helped Catholics to discover that much more was needed in terms of content and methods of religious education than mere control of the schools. They saw that renewal had to be within themselves first if they were to have an impact on the religious training of the children. Hence, from 1962 onwards, there were several talks, seminars and courses for priests, religious and lay-teachers of religion. Already from 1955 the Ceylon national seminary under the Oblates of Mary Immaculate had been sending out young priests with a more renewed theology and a greater openness to the world. Aquinas University College in

Colombo was another centre of continuing renewal of Catholic thinking. This openness was, however, uneven with reference to geographical areas and subject-matter. Dioceses like Kandy and Colombo were more open, whereas Jaffna diocese had been conspicuous by its official closedness to new thinking, even after Vatican II.

During this period there was severe criticism of Catholics in the country, especially in the public press. Catholics were accused of being disloyal to the country, and conspirators for their own self-advancement. It was only gradually that the rest of the country began to understand that a change was taking place within the Catholic group.

Efforts at Renewal, 1965

Vatican II, the election of a more right-wing government, and the passage of time helped Catholics to reconcile themselves to the rest of the country, and vice versa. As the new government was more disposed to foster inter-religious amity, public criticism of Catholics almost completely disappeared in the years after 1965. For the first time, Catholics did not oppose a bill in favour of Buddhists and against their apparent interests: the conversion of the weekly holiday from Sunday to the lunar "poya day". This indicated a clear change in the attitude of the Catholic group; although critics suggested that this was due to the right-wing policies of the government. In the meantime the seminars and discussions continued. In January 1965, Father Lombardi and his "Better World" team conducted a week's retreat with discussions for five hundred persons from the whole church. It created much hopes of a forward movement together. After 1965 renewal courses were intensified, especially for religious. Aquinas University College provided many such courses, and published "Quest"—a journal devoted to the renewal of the Church in Ceylon. The bishops established post-Vatican II commissions for liturgy, catechetics, other religions, non-believers, and so on. These functioned rather haphazardly, except for the catechetics commission.

Kandy diocese held a diocesan synod—the first and so far only one of its kind in Ceylon; the laity and religious participated in the deliberations. At Easter 1966 the conference of bishops decided to hold a national synod at Pentecost 1968. The synod deliberations, for which representatives of the religious, priests and laity made suggestions, resulted in a sort of compromise regarding the policy of the church, although controversial issues, such as relations with Marxism and Buddhism, were glossed over. The national synod was an advance in so far as it meant a theoretical affirmation by the church in Ceylon of the Vatican II concepts of the Church, its mission and relationships within it. The decisions of the synod were eventually approved by Rome in 1970 and now await implementation both in the spirit and to a great extent in the letter.

Leadership closes in

In very recent years the leadership of the church has seemed to be rather wary of or even opposed to changes in the direction of openness to the world. This is due to the consolidation of the right-wing government from 1965–1970, the trends of the Church in Rome, and the apprehension among local leaders about the trends in North America and Europe, especially the crisis in the priestly and religious ranks. *Humanae Vitae* and its aftermath also helped to confirm the leaders in a more conservative stance. The new bishops appointed in the last few years do not confirm the hope that changes would come from the top. A more conservative tendency is enforcing itself on the organizations and agencies of the church. Commissions such as those for catechetics, liturgy, biblical work, educations were reappointed or constituted in such a way that more forward-looking persons hardly found a place in them. The Catholic press owned by the church as well as periodicals published by Catholic groups began to feel the pressure of official disapproval of more open approaches. In the meantime the more reform minded groups too have become more radicalized. Lay journals (*Outlook* in English and *Jana Randa* in Sinhala) begun in more recent years were forthright in their critique of the church and of churchmen. With the influx of younger teachers who had been in Rome during the days of the Council, the national seminary too seems to have become more radicalized.

Difficulties within the church seem to be increasing. In the diocese of Chilaw, an apostolic visitor had to be appointed to iron out serious divergences between forty priests and the bishops supported by some other priests. During the past few years about twenty priests out of the six hundred or so have left the priesthood; there is a similar exodus among religious brothers and sisters. The mental alienation among those who serve the church, including laymen, is very much more serious than this exodus.

Changes in Society

The re-election of the left-wing coalition under Mrs Bandaranaike in May 1970 made the church authorities and Catholics rethink their policies. A good number of Catholics supported the leftward trend both ideologically and with the vote. This was a very significant change from the early nineteen-sixties. The more right-wing Catholics of the establishment of both church and society had to adjust themselves to the new socialistic climate. The armed insurrection of youth in April 1971 shocked the elder generation to an awareness of the depth of its alienation from young people. This has further radicalized the younger element within the church. Recently sixty-one younger priests sent the public press a memorandum which they submitted to the Roman Synod recommending greater relevance of the priestly life to social justice, the acceptance of a married clergy and the ordination of women to certain grades of the ministry. A heated debate is now on in the public press.

The difference of opinion between the national seminary staff and the bishops' conference had led to the decree of the bishops to take over the national seminary from the Oblates with effect from the next academic year. This is likely to create further tensions within the church. The seminarians, too, have been agitating for reforms in their life style, and the content and methods of their studies. These have so far not led to any very significant change because the bishops are unwilling to experiment too much with priestly vocations. Meanwhile, the number and quality of vocations has decreased, and some of the more energetic seminarians have left the seminary. The bishops think this is due to the "laxity" of the seminarists, while the more reform-minded attribute it to the slowness of the leadership to adapt themselves to change. The overall polarization within the church is now building up to serious proportions and affects all groups.

Assessment: A Changed Church

The changes in the world, the country and the universal Church have combined to bring about more changes in the church in Ceylon during the past ten years than in the previous century.

Trials and tensions have helped to bring about a creative re-thinking and a partial adaptation. The public image of the church as a whole has changed considerably; it is no longer monolithic, anti-socialistic, opposed to the aspiration of the Buddhists, Hindus and Muslims (not to mention other Christians), or of the Sinhalese and Tamils as cultural groups. Catholics are no longer so cocksure of themselves either as possessors of *the* truth or controllers of the unique means of salvation. A certain self-critique is taking place; for example, the hierarchy commissioned a socio-religious survey by Canon François Houtart and his team from Louvain.[1]

The structures of the Church of Vatican II have been set up: commissions, secretariats, etc.; though these are mainly nominated. The bishops' conference is meeting more often and for longer periods; it is becoming a sort of executive. The religious congregations are updating themselves and the lay organizations are partially renewed. The shock of the loss of the schools has been absorbed, and the church as a whole is better related to the country; the tensions are more within the church itself.

Changes Inadequate

The country has moved ahead much further than the church, and a new generation of youth is impatient with the establishment in both the country and the church. On the other hand the leadership in the church has remained the same during the past twenty-five years and seems to have reached the limits of its preparedness to change. This is true of the older laity who control the Catholic Union of Ceylon and certain lay organizations. Much will depend in the future on the younger bishops who will be at the helm in four to five years, assuming that the four older

[1] Cf. "Quest 43", Centre for Religion and Society, Talahena, Malabe, Ceylon, for summary of Survey Report; and SEDEC, Archbishop's House Colombo 8 for full mimeographed report.

bishops will retire at seventy-five years of age. So far the younger bishops have not shown much initiative and leadership. The religious superiors can be a very important balancing force in the church of tomorrow. In any case the church in Ceylon is set for a grave internal crisis within the next six to seven years, if not earlier. The young are asserting themselves and the old order is not showing itself adequately dynamic and pliable. The church in Ceylon has had a most valuable experience in self-reform; yet it has a long way to go before being in the mainstream of the country. It has very great potential; much will depend on the course of world events and on its internal vitality.

Biographical Notes

YVES CONGAR, O.P., was born in 1904 in Sedan (France) and ordained in 1930. In 1969 he published *L'Ecclésiologie du haut moyen âge* and a new edition of *Vraie et fausse réforme dans l'Eglise* (1st edn., 1950). He edited the section dealing with the period from St Augustine to the present day of the history of ecclesiological doctrines which forms part of the *Dogmengeschichte* published by Herder. In the *Unam Sanctam* series which he founded and still directs he has brought out detailed commentaries on the texts of Vatican II with the aid of numerous experts. He is a member of the International Theological Commission.

ADOLF EXELER was born 15 February 1926 in Rheine, Westphalia, and ordained in 1951. He studied at the University of Münster. Doctor of theology, he is professor of pastoral theology at the University of Münster. Among his published works are: *Die neue Gemeinde* (Mainz, 1966) and *Glaube an Jesus, den Christ* (Fribourg im B., 1968).

ADRIAN HASTINGS was born in June 1929 in Kuala Lumpur and ordained in 1955. He studied history at Oxford and theology in Rome. Master of arts and doctor of theology, he has worked in Africa since 1958. Among his published works are a commentary in two volumes on the documents of Vatican II and a book of essays, *Mission and Ministry* (London, 1971).

INGO HERMANN was born 23 January 1932 in Bocholt (Germany). He studied at the Universities of Münster, Munich and Innsbruck. Doctor of theology, he is head of the department of educational programmes of the second television channel in Germany. Among his published works are: *Kommentar zum Markusevangelium* (1965 and 1967) and *Die Christen und ihre Konflickte* (1970).

PETER HUIZING, S.J., was born 22 January 1911 in Haarlem and ordained in 1942. He studied at the Universities of Amsterdam, Nijmegen and Louvain and at the Gregorian (Rome). Licentiate of philosophy and of theology, doctor of civil and canon law, he is professor of canon law and of the history of canon law at the University of Nijmegen. He is also a consultor to the Pontifical Commission for the Revision of the Code of Canon Law. Among his published works is *De Trentse huwelijksvorm* (Hilversum/Antwerp, 1966).

ALOIS MÜLLER was born 20 September 1924 in Basle and ordained in 1949. He studied at the University of Fribourg, at the Angelicum (Rome) and at the Higher Institute of Catechetics (Paris). Doctor of theology, he is professor of pastoral theology at the University of Fribourg. Among his published works are: *Die neue Kirche und die Erziehung* (1966), which has been translated into English, French and Hungarian, and *Kirchenreform heute* (1968).

KARL-HEINZ OHLIG was born 15 September 1938 in Koblenz (Germany). He studied at the Universities of Trèves, Innsbruck and Münster. Doctor of theology, he is professor of Catholic theology and religious pedagogy at the High School of Pedagogy in Saarbrücken. Among his published works are: *Woher nimmt die Bibel ihre Autorität?* (1970) and, with H. Schuster, *Blockiert das katholische Dogma die Einheit der Kirchen?* (1971).

THOMAS F. O'DEA was born 1 December 1915 in Amesbury (U.S.A.) and is a Catholic. He studied at Harvard University. Master of arts and doctor of philosophy, he is professor of sociology and of religious studies and director of the Institute of Religious Studies at the University of California, Santa Barbara. Among his published works are: *The Catholic Crisis* (Boston, ²1969) and *Sociology and the Study of Religion* (New York, 1970).

STEPHAN PFÜRTNER, O.P., was born 23 November 1922 in Danzig. He studied at the Universities of Breslau, Kiel and Fribourg and in Rome. Doctor of theology, he is professor of moral theology at the University of Fribourg. Among his published works are: *Triebleben und sittliche Vollendung* (Fribourg, 1958), and *Luther und Thomas im Gespräch. Unser Heil zwischen Gewissheit und Gefährdung* (Heidelberg, 1961).

International Publishers of CONCILIUM

ENGLISH EDITION
Herder and Herder Inc.
New York, U.S.A.

Burns & Oates Ltd.
P.O. Box 497,
London, S.W.7

DUTCH EDITION
Uitgeverij Paul Brand, N.V.
Hilversum, Netherlands

FRENCH EDITION
Maison Mame
Tours/Paris, France

JAPANESE EDITION (PARTIAL)
Nansôsha
Tokyo, Japan

GERMAN EDITION
Verlagsanstalt Benziger & Co., A.G.
Einsiedeln, Switzerland

Matthias Grunewald-Verlag
Mainz, W. Germany

SPANISH EDITION
Ediciones Cristianidad
Salamanca, Spain

PORTUGUESE EDITION
Livraria Morais Editoria, Ltda.
Lisbon, Portugal

ITALIAN EDITION
Editrice Queriniana
Brescia, Italy

POLISH EDITION (PARTIAL)
Pallottinum
Poznań, Poland